CRYSTAL CLEAR

CRYSTAL CLEAR

Reflections on Extraordinary Talismans for Everyday Life

JAYA SAXENA

QUIRK BOOKS

PHILADELPHIA

Library of Congress Cataloging in Publication Data
Saxena, Jaya, author.
Crystal clear: reflections on extraordinary talismans
for everyday life / Jaya Saxena.
Summary: "Personal essays about the self-care
applications of crystals"—Provided by publisher.
LCSH: Crystals—Miscellanea.
BF1442.C78 S39 2020 | DDC 133/.2548—dc23
2020031963

ISBN: 978-1-68369-203-4

Printed in China
Typeset in Brandon Grotesque, Manofa, Recoleta, and Sabon

Designed by Andie Reid
Illustrations by Vero Escalante
Production management by John J. McGurk

Quirk Books
215 Church Street
Philadelphia, PA 19106
quirkbooks.com

10 9 8 7 6 5 4 3 2 1

For every kid who
picked up a rock
and saw more than
just dirt

CONTENTS

INTRODUCTION

"What unnatural words. Always and forever! Those aren't human words, Jim. Not even stones are always and forever."

—Mary Doria Russell, *The Sparrow*

When you think of marble you probably think of it in its most basic, everyday forms: as a countertop, a kitchen backsplash, or a floor if you frequent slightly more luxe apartments. It's a material that's considered opulent but also recedes into the background. Even at the Taj Mahal, it's not the marble itself that people marvel at; it's the way it's carved and inlaid—and the fact that there's just so much of it. Marble is luxurious but it's also durable; as much at home in a cathedral or a palace as it is in a hardware catalog. In other words: marble is nothing special.

But the California Crystal Cave in Sequoia National Park, a living structure of marble and calcite, will make you feel like an alien on your own planet. As I stood outside the cave on a midsummer day, looking at the spiderwebbed gate that led to the cavern's tunnels, I felt a breeze thirty degrees cooler emanate from the entrance, touching my cheek like a ghost beckoning me inside. My partner, Matt, and I were there for a discovery tour, conducted only with flashlights. Over the course of a million years, water had been inching its way across a solid piece of marble inside a mountain, dissolving it bit by bit, sculpting entire rooms in its wake. It's a magnificent natural structure; the supernatural need not apply.

I was never interested in crystals in a metaphysical or spiritual way. I was always drawn to their reality—their solidity. In a childhood diary, I bragged about my rock collection; pyrite, marble, raw emerald, and smoky quartz that I kept in a seashell-decorated, heart-shaped box. I opened it every night, removing each one by one to admire them, and then puzzling them all back so the lid could shut. In 1992, when I was six years old, I had sixty-two specimens, and big books with big pictures telling me where the rocks were likely mined, and what their practical uses were. Quartz was used in making computers, diamond to cut hard metals, crushed pearls to lend makeup an iridescent quality. In my diary I recorded which were my favorites—one day hematite, another limestone. I liked the way they glittered, the way they felt, how some seemed too light for their size and others too heavy, some sharp and some waxy, and how there could be such variance to what were essentially condensed forms of dirt. These stones didn't need to have otherworldly properties in order to be valuable. They were fascinating on their own.

Inside the Crystal Cave, there are marble formations that look like a snowdrift, like popcorn or organ pipes. There are white calcite formations that look like the folds of a human brain. There are basins full of clear water called "Fairy Pools" that show a calcite lattice, like the most sturdy and elegant caul fat, beneath its undisturbed surface. Marble reaches out like the mangled claws of spirits trying to escape a dark prison. You could watch your breath becoming vapor in the path of a flashlight. I felt as close to magic as I've ever been.

At one point we were asked by our guide, Michelle, to sit in the dark in total silence and listen to the sounds of the cave—water dropping, echoing, some sense of coolness and space the silence only amplified. It seemed natural that people who stumbled into this formation before flashlights and paved trails wanted to take this energy with them, to have a physical remnant to connect them back to this massive formation. Perhaps when they saw the calcite chip stolen from the cavern wall, no matter how out of context, they would remember how it felt to be wholly absorbed by the earth. In the darkness, any theoretical power of the stones around me became immediately obvious.

"Nature" has come to mean something very specific in mainstream understanding, namely, something to save. It's dying, after all, and we're the ones killing it. Animals are becoming extinct, coral reefs are drying up, the seas are increasingly inhospitable, and the forests are being cut down. Even without human intervention, these forms of nature change all the time. Animals eat each other, trees dry out and rebloom, rivers push into new courses. But a rock, a mountain, is dark and craggy and rough, ready to kill you. It used to be that mountains inspired terror instead of admiration, back when nature was something to prepare against, not something to consume. You could die on a mountain (people still die on mountains), but even if you didn't, you would die anyway, and the mountain would remain. These formations are not changing at a scale a human can understand.

Crystals are nature. Crystals—the shiny, multicolored gems and crystalline structures we speak of here—are born of pressure in the earth and die by eventual erosion. "In a crystal we have clear evidence of the existence of a formative life principle, and though we cannot understand the life of a crystal, it is nonetheless a living being," wrote Nikola Tesla in his essay "The Problem of Increasing Human Energy," published in 1900. Crystals are not permanent, but they live outside of human time. Rocks, supposedly, are doing fine without us. Which is exactly why we want them.

A friend asked me where our theories about crystals come from, and if they were all invented in the 1960s by hippies who just discovered chakras. In reality, descriptions of the properties of gemstones have existed for centuries, before we had the science to differentiate mineral structures and elemental compositions. Which is why, metaphysically, "gems" is a category that includes pearl, amber, coral, and petrified wood. It was a matter of finding the fantastic in the earth, regardless of what architecture their molecules might have.

Pliny the Elder wrote of both the healing and supposed mystical powers of gems in *The Natural History* in 79 AD. "I find it stated by medical men that the very best cautery for the human body is a ball of crystal acted upon by the rays of the sun," he wrote. In this work, he was building on Peripatetic philosopher Theophrastus's work *On Stones*, an early encyclopedic source on rocks and gems that made note of phenomena like pyroelectricity and magnetism.

Saint Hildegard von Bingen, a twelfth-century nun and philosopher who wrote about medicine and physiology, and who preached about God's presence in what most of her contemporaries considered a mystical way, wrote in her *Physica* that gemstones contain "energy and moisture" and that their power comes from where they absorbed those elements from, sending waves and rays into the bodies of those who used them. This, she preached, was God's hand. "[Gemstones] terrify the devil, who hates and despises them because he remembered that their beauty appeared in him before he fell from the glory which God had given him," she wrote.

In Hinduism, nine stones are said to ward against the powers of the nine planets.

In thirteenth-century Italy, Peter Apon of Padua, an ordinary citizen who claimed to have seven spirits inside a crystal, was executed by Inquisitors for being a magician. (His death was noted by Francis Hutchinson, a British minister in Bury St. Edmunds in England who deconstructed witch hunts and witchcraft prosections in "An Historical Essay Concerning Witchcraft.")

Li Shizhen, a sixteenth-century physician in China during the Ming Dynasty, suggested using jade and amber to treat wounds and quartz for thirst and cough.

"How comes it that man in all times and conditions has agreed to hold gems worshipful?" asked ethnologist J. M. Campbell in an 1896 issue of the journal *Indian Antiquary.* "How is it that the sickly doubting beryl spirit of the Thomases not less than the trusting full blooded jasper spirit of the Peters have found magic and mystic influences in gems?" He posits it's because gems hold guardian spirits, but the question remains. Most of these texts, no matter how early, accepted the power of gemstones as truth. These philosophers and scientists and mystics all turn into bumbling high school students while discussing crystals, beginning their arguments with "since the dawn of time" and never showing instead of telling. And now, most modern crystal guides and sources consider these powers as old as human thought, though none can point to who first decided that amethysts were good for spiritual balance.

As I write this, there's an increased interest in the powers of crystals, another crest on a sine wave that can be traced from the mesmerism of the Victorian era, which gave us the image of a woman in a head scarf with a crystal ball, through the séance craze of the 1920s, to the Age of Aquarius. In the 1970s the New Age movement arose to carry the torch of '60s counterculture and rebellion, morphing from a (sometimes irresponsible) cultural curiosity about what existed outside of white, Christian America into a marketing plan for anything that smacked of foreign-ness and self-healing.

By the '80s, crystals were everywhere as the New Age movement was further diluted. Claire's, the iconic accessories store for girls, was filled with "buddha bead" bracelets of varying stones, each with an accompanying card explaining what kind of luck your jewelry will bring. Just as you could buy key chains and underwear with your zodiac sign, you could sift through a set of adjustable rings sporting birthstones. Every museum gift shop sold gem collections glued to a piece of cardboard. Trolls had "gems" instead of belly buttons, and Polly Pocket had an entire line of miniature homes decorated with plastic rhinestones meant to stand in for the real thing. The omnipresence of crystals in malls and tourist stops made young adults all the more ready to reconnect with them. However, they were mostly marketed toward young girls, and then easily dismissed as being childish, frivolous toys, a trend for the unserious. Few probably thought to steer these rock-obsessed girls toward geology.

Though I wasn't initially occupied with the mystical properties of crystals, I also wasn't immune to their magic growing up in the '80s and '90s. I got my first crystals at every New York kid's ultimate field trip destination, the American Museum of Natural History, where I waited patiently every time until we got to the Morgan Memorial Hall of Gems and Minerals. The room was dark and musty, with carpeted walls and low lights. The teachers never seemed to think rocks were as important as dinosaurs or early hominids, so we were often left to wander by ourselves. We could touch formations of petrified rock and amethyst geodes. In one room was a collection of stones glowing with radiation. There were cut gems fit for any piece of jewelry, but also columns and crags of multicolored rock that could never be made more beautiful by human interference. Some kids sat on the stairs while others snuck into dark corners to make out. But I was struck by the powerful fact that we were surrounded not just by nature but by beauty.

"The door to the American Museum of Natural History's new Hall of Minerals and Gems is like the mouth of a fabulous cave," wrote Boyce Renberger in the *New York Times* in 1976. It was overseen by Dr. Vincent Manson, a consultant to the museum, to be interactive and to evoke feeling, not just intellectual curiosity. Though the stones were labeled, there wasn't much explanation as to how the crystals were formed, of the volcanic and tectonic movements of the earth, of how a gray rock turns into a pink gem. Instead, Manson wanted kids to slide down a slope of jade. He wanted people to touch the rocks, "put their arms around them, fall in love with them," he said. "We want minerals to come across not only as scientific documents but as art objects, as objects of aesthetic value that anyone can look at and see the beauties of the earth." For all my rock collecting, I still didn't know much about how stones were made. And I didn't care, because the Hall of Gems and Minerals validated the feelings I felt when I held my own collection of crystals. As a kid in New York I had often looked down to see mica shimmering in the granite sidewalk and pretended I was walking across an enchanted river, but this felt bigger, like something outside of me. I became skeptical of the rest of the museum; who could possibly be entranced by leaves and skin and fur when the entire spectrum of color and beauty was lying cold and pulseless beneath your feet?

The museum gift shop sold crystals of all kinds, a piece of the room to take home with you. There were big vats of colored stones you could stick your hand into and feel like you were being sucked in, pre-packaged collections of stones with information about where they came from, and beautiful earrings and key chains. I always saved my money for the geodes, which held the promise that a formation as beautiful as one in any museum lay inside. I'd take one back to my apartment, stuff it in a tube sock, and wail on it with a hammer until it cracked. I marveled every time at the crumbled surprises inside and thought about how sometimes science and magic feel like the same thing, how there could be beauty in the former and order in the latter. I let myself open to the possibility of not just knowledge, but wonder.

But it was never quite the same as being surrounded by structures bigger than myself. I couldn't be overwhelmed by something I had such power over.

⌄⌄⌄⌄

Now, in another time of political turmoil and rebellion, crystals have woven themselves back into everyday life. The "crystal industry" is booming again, and Google searches for "crystal healing" have skyrocketed in the past few years. And they've become even more mainstream. You can buy a glass water bottle with a rose quartz inside to cleanse your water, a jade yoni egg, or just a handful of gems at Urban Outfitters or Target. Once upon a time, you would have had to go to a museum or a New Age store on the edge of town. But now it is not uncommon for someone to know the properties of a few popular crystals the way they might know their zodiac sign.

Whether or not you're nostalgic for spending all your allowance on mood rings and tiger's-eye, crystals can be a way to connect back to the tangible, practical elements of our life. Crystal healer Colleen McCann told *Fast Company* in 2017 this is because, as a people, we are stressed out, and for all of our technological and capitalistic advances, most people's problems have gotten worse. And, at least in America, both mental and physical health care are inaccessible for many. Touching something that comes from the earth calms us, McCann says, and right now we need as much of that as we can get. I know that a rock can't make me rich. But what feels closer to essential is the things we want these stones to represent. Crystals may not have carried supernatural energy "since the dawn of time," but since around then, humans have ascribed meaning, however arbitrary, to objects that appeal to us. And really, there are only a few things these stones ever channel—love, confidence, serenity, the power to receive the good or block out the bad. We assign these properties because they're the things we wish we had control over.

This all sounded ridiculous to me for most of my life. I was raised knowing *of* religions—my grandparents' Hinduism, my school's Quakerism, my friends' and spouse's Judaism—but I landed with my dad's atheism. That's still largely where I stand, but there's something about the storytelling behind some spiritual practices that I can't help but be allured by. I've opened my mind enough to the supernatural to incorporate elements of it into my life, the vocabulary of which changes depending on who you ask. Some people call it witchcraft or just being indecisive. Most often it feels to me like curiosity balanced with skepticism—a willingness to pick up new ideas, but not without analyzing them first.

I understand the force of nature that crystals evoke. But I had never subjected myself to crystal healing, and the idea that these crystals could be used for my specific, immediate benefit. I knew the power of tarot, which is essentially a cheap version of therapy using sequential art to trick you into admitting what you already know, but the vibe I got from crystal healers was that they believed the rocks could pull the bad humors out of your body. I started noticing just how many opportunities for crystal healing there were around New York City, neon signs reading PSYCHIC in second-story windows with accompanying sidewalk sandwich boards offering a look into a crystal ball for $5. Surely this was a scam.

But of course I had to do it. I chose a "center for healing" in Greenpoint, Brooklyn, an upscale, airy space that offered crystal healing sessions along with sound baths, astrocartography workshops, acupuncture, and, on the evening I visited, laughing yoga classes. You essentially enter through the gift shop. Blond wood tables displayed artfully curated piles of crystals, each with a card espousing the stones' origin, properties, and associated zodiac signs. (In a store, a bowl of tumbled rose quartz looks the same as a pile of mancala beads, or the stones you buy by the pound at the pet store to line the bottom of your aquarium.) In the absence of the overwhelming presence of a cave or the weird darkness of a museum, you have to be told how to feel about them. And if you don't already assume the stones are magical, it's not self-evident.

I ran my hands over the other things on display. Most were guides telling you how to use everything on sale. There were crystal bibles with in-depth descriptions of their powers and guides to navigating one's chakras. There were eye masks shaped to simulate Reiki hands and aromatherapeutic oils and sprays. Everything was cute. In keeping with the vision of Dr. Manson, everything was chosen for its aesthetic value. But instead of emulating a cave or a natural formation, the store emulated the lifestyle it was selling. You, too, can be an earth goddess. All you have to do is buy the right rock.

My crystal healing started out like a tarot reading, where the crystals I drew were supposed to illuminate the subconscious state of my life and allow me to get in touch with what I needed. My crystal healer for the evening, who was the picture of earthly beauty with long, radiant hair and an abundance of freckles, sat me in a chair. She placed herself across from me, and between us was a table full of crystals covered with a gauzy blanket. I closed my eyes as she dimmed the lights and led me through a meditation, after which I was to open my eyes and choose whichever stones appealed to me. When I opened my eyes they darted to the right. Things were still pretty blurry but I saw color struggling to shine in the dim candlelight. I knew most of the crystals on the table—a round tiger's-eye the shape of a duck egg, a thin selenite wand, a smattering of quartzes and calcites of different colors—but I figured the whole point of this was to go with what drew me, and I picked an oversized, multicolored piece and two daintier stones.

My healer informed me that I had chosen a titanium quartz, a malachite, and an ocean jasper. She found this fascinating, though she probably would have said that no matter what I chose. The combination of these three signaled to her that I was in a new, joyous state. Exciting things were happening, and to make the most of them I had to stay buoyant but calm and work on connecting my creativity to my joy and not my anxiety. Which, as a lifelong try-hard who can't stand having a deadline hanging over her head, made me feel quite seen.

The rest of the session continued with Reiki healing. She placed my chosen crystals on my body and her hands all over my chakras, I think. As I breathed, I felt the stones threaten to roll off my belly, and felt that specific satisfaction of having been game for something new, no matter how silly it looked from the outside. But then, as she moved her hands to my ribs, I felt my skin flutter and twitch. I figured it was internal, possibly gas. She couldn't have known. But at the end, she mentioned it too. I was "fizzing" around there, possibly a sign that my creative self and my compassionate self were having a hard time communicating. Essentially, I wasn't appreciating myself enough, and it was manifesting in my rumbling organs. It was the sort of vague prediction that makes newspaper horoscopes feel mostly real. Like yeah, I probably wasn't, but who does?

I felt relaxed and clearheaded afterward, though I couldn't tell if it was the crystals or just the sensation of lying with my eyes closed in a dim room for an hour. On my way out, she told me I really should have a malachite and pointed to a cluster of them near the register. I assured her I had one at home, and she kissed me on the cheek and went on to her next client. At the register, the cashier asked if I wanted to get anything else besides the healing. Maybe one of the stones that had been used on me, if I wanted to take a look?

▰▰▰▰▰

Supposedly one reason we like glittery gemstones is because the gleam of their crystalline or mineraloid structures reminds us of how light scatters on water. They're as close to objective beauty as we can get. And from another angle, assigning power to beauty allows us to be closer to it. Much of magic is based in the ability to extend metaphor to physical objects—a burned herb that cleanses a space, a lock of hair kept in a notebook, a religious symbol on a chain around your neck that reminds you of the meaning you put in it. But when you burn an herb there's nothing left. Crystals and gemstones feel like forever. As far away from the cave as you are, they feel permanent in a way other magical objects often don't, a reminder of ancient formations and, possibly, objects that carry carbon pieces of our ancestors with them. They are harder, more resilient, more beautiful things made of the same stuff as us. Of course we would want them to carry all our hopes for love and success and psychic protection. They are strong enough to not be undone by desire.

A spell is just a story. To cast one, you are forced to say your wishes out loud, to imagine what would happen to you if you got what you wanted and ask the universe to make it so. Most of us have so many desires, small and large, filtering through us all the time, and we externalize those desires by assigning them to crystals and gems because otherwise, we might forget that occasionally we need to focus on our passions, or be more generous with those we love, or let the light in. But what's more, we tell these stories with crystals and incense and chants because we want to create ourselves. To make other people see us and treat us the way we want them to, we have to see ourselves that way first. To look at a gem that we have assigned the role of creativity, or peace, or money, means that there's a version of the story in which we have it. It's happening right now. It's in your hand.

▼▲▼▲

The immediate draw of crystals may be that they are fixed and hard representations of everything we want, but some of the subconscious appeal is that no matter how permanent they feel, they, too, can change. Growth is not just the provenance of blooming flowers and birthed children, but the slow, nearly unnoticeable work of building a glittering cave, iota by iota, that results in something more magnificent than any story you could have imagined. We can change toward the things we want. Even the hardest parts of us are not static.

My favorite stone isn't one I bought in a witch shop or museum. I picked it up on the beach in New Jersey during a brief respite to an emotional summer, my partner and I walking along the sand in the late afternoon while my dad and his dogs ran in the surf ahead. It's translucent with bands of white running through it, sized like a flat robin's egg, and sanded enough to feel like the skin on my earlobe.

It is possibly a type of quartz, or maybe a white agate. I don't know, because it doesn't really matter. What matters is how it reminds me of standing on the beach in late summer when you start to feel the first pricklings of autumn air, the taste of wine in a plastic cup and the pale sting of almost-forgotten mosquito bites, the feeling of completion and slight loss as you recognize that the sun has started to set earlier and earlier. I am reminded of peace. I feel content and aware, an expansive version of myself, the entirety of my capability of feeling and under-standing and grace, the stone a thing grounding me to an idea I'm sure I've already had but now feel with my whole body.

I cherish my stone collection not because I believe they will lend me their secrets, but because they are a reminder of all the work I've done to change for the better, and all the work I've yet to do. I do not believe in the inherent power of any of these stones. But I do believe there's a reason why we created representations for the powers they represent, and that by analyzing those myths and texts and desires, we can make them more powerful. Their power may be arbitrary, but since when has that been a barometer of meaning? The magic is not in the stones, but knowing why we are externalizing these metaphors, why someone would look outside themselves for love or protection, and why certain desires feel so universal. The magic is in an object turning into a placeholder for emotion, regardless of whether that emotion lines up with what the crystal guides say it represents, and in turn making you more aware of and beholden to that feeling. And the magic is in evoking the feeling of a cave you will probably never enter, but some part of you knowing what it would be like to be completely surrounded by nature, a small chip of a whole that, against all odds, you have the power to change.

The
ROSE
QUARTZ
Ceiling of
Unconditional
Love

Rose Quartz

DESCRIPTION:

A type of quartz (a crystalline mineral) with a pale pink or rosy hue; smooth and translucent, with a waxy texture

COMPOSITION:

Silicon dioxide (SiO_2)

METAPHYSICAL PROPERTIES:

Invokes a deep feeling of universal love and connection; restores trust and harmony in friendships; allows one the power to give and receive love

The Millennial women in my life love Baz Luhrmann's 2001 film *Moulin Rouge!*. Most of us were teenagers when it was released, the perfect age to be taken in by corsets and Paris and Ewan McGregor's bangs, as well as its cartoonish understanding of love and sex. It didn't matter that literally every man in the movie was setting Nicole Kidman's character, Satine, up to fail, ignoring her reluctance and her pleas that, really, a roof over her head and career opportunities would help her out a lot more than love. But love—exclamation point love!—was the grandest and most beautiful pursuit, according to the men—and to the little girls watching at home. It was the thing we wanted most: big and red and expressed through song. Even now, I feel my skin about to burst when I hear the film's ultimate message (a lyric from "Nature Boy," first recorded by Nat King Cole): "The greatest thing you'll ever learn is just to love and be loved in return."

To not only love but accept love, to swirl and dance in its pink mist—what else could you want out of life? What greater thing could there be to experience? Sure, I knew people who rolled their eyes at the corny and overwhelming score, at the baseness of the lesson. "Love is good? Is that all?" And my friends and I rolled our eyes back, because yes, it *was* all. It is all. It's everything.

But with some distance from the big emotions of adolescence, I recognize a sadness in the film's message. The only characters who sing that line are men—lovestruck, idealistic men who are championed for being emotionally open. Satine, the woman who was the object of their desire, dies without ever having achieved her dreams, all the love in the world unable to save her. Now I realize that we were absorbing the text and the subtext: the greatest thing we're expected to do is love and be loved in return—no matter what else we, as women, might want to accomplish. These are the heights to which we're expected to aspire. Men who love are enlightened beings, heroes of musicals, takers of action against all odds. But women aren't celebrated for the act of loving others because we've been socially conditioned to believe that women are born to love—and present themselves as objects to be loved in return. If we believe that love is a woman's default setting, baked into her DNA, then we leave no room for her to feel angry, to hate, to prefer her own companionship to that of a romantic partner, and—god forbid—to choose a life without children. And so we hit the rose quartz ceiling.

▼▲▼▲▼

If you've ever been curious about crystals, you probably have a rose quartz. Unlike diamonds and pearls, which typically belong in the jewelry box and are worn purely for adornment, rose quartz is utilitarian. It's the starter crystal for any budding witch, ubiquitous in museum shops and magic stores. Even if you're not interested in witchcraft or metaphysics, it's an easy stone to dabble with, and is on the same level as reading your horoscope or getting a casual tarot reading. Even people who find these self-divinatory pratices illogical can own a rose quartz and think, What's the harm? While other stones may promise money or luck or protection from some unseen enemy, rose quartz promises to fulfill the most universal desire—love—which makes it immediately appealing. Love is deemed a necessity more than a luxury, which justifies a pursuit by any means, but it's also never guaranteed. There is no direct action you can take to obtain or maintain love, nothing that will make love happen. When there's no other option for bringing love into your life, the rose quartz starts to make sense. If you can't control it, maybe some unseen, misunderstood energies can.

I bought my rose quartz at House of Intuition in Los Angeles during a weeklong vacation between ending one job and beginning another. I was drained, looking for a stone or two to keep at my new desk and serve as a reminder to not lose myself; to work hard, but keep myself happy, to remember that the whole point of work was to enjoy the life it could provide outside of work. I don't remember what the little card in the shop said about rose quartz, but on their website, at the time of this writing, it reads: "Stone of universal love. Strengthens and balances the heart. Brings comfort in time of grief. Encourages forgiveness and invokes self-trust." I posted my crystals on Instagram after I bought them, saying the rose quartz was to "protect my heart."

I'm not sure if I would have bought it if its description used the language I've found most other places. One website calls it "feminine in tone and one of the stones of the Great Mother." Another says it imparts "warm, loving, feminine energy." Yet another calls it one of

While interpretations of crystals can vary from source to source, the rose quartz is always the stone of unconditional love.

the most "versatile feminine stones," which you can use to honor your "divine feminine." Even when sources don't explicitly call out the feminine, they say the stone promotes love, generosity, and compassion and is supposed to aid in childbirth. It's not hard to figure out who this is meant for. While interpretations of crystals can vary from source to source, the rose quartz is always the stone of unconditional love. Its pale pink translucence is said to pull at the heart and fill you with light and softness; to remind you of your love for others and your love for yourself. It also "carries a soft feminine energy," as opposed to the "masculine," aggressive energy of other stones. Some witchcraft traditions have subbed in "passive and active" energies for "feminine and masculine," but in a society that places those concepts firmly in a gender binary, we know which is which.

Whether or not you identify as a woman or in any way feminine, to associate the binary of love and hate with any other binary assumes that love is naturally accessible only to some and requires a leap for others. Even the most generous reading of the crystal's properties, which say we all have both masculine and feminine energies in us, still buys into the existence of a dichotomy. Rose quartz promises love, but it is only in the supposedly "feminine" way—passive, unconditional, existing vaguely in the ether, radiating an energy that inspires people to sing love songs about them. A woman offers herself up to love and reciprocates it; she is a vessel, ready and waiting to be filled, and to return that love to all who expect it from her. All of these descriptions point to the feminine. And it is always the feminine side of any duality that is expected to sacrifice, to give without condition, and to absorb without resistance.

▼▲▼▲▼

Rose quartz was born of a woman's tears and a man's blood. In Greek mythology, goddess Aphrodite and mortal Adonis were lovers, soul mates in love and renewal and beauty. In Ovid's telling, Aphrodite warns Adonis of hunting for sport, "lest your glory may cost me great sorrow . . . lest courage should be fatal to us both." But he ignores her wishes for him to be cautious and attacks a boar. Some versions of the myth say the boar was sent by a jealous Ares, the god of war and Aphrodite's former lover. Others say Artemis sent the boar. But in every version Adonis chooses his glory and courage over the wishes of his lover.

Whatever happened, by the time Aphrodite arrived, she found her mortal love bleeding out. In *Metamorphoses*, Ovid writes that the red anemone, or a rose, sprung from the earth where Adonis's blood fell. Some modern versions of the myth say it was rose quartz that was formed by his blood mixed with Aphrodite's tears, and the stone is a symbol of their eternal union—forever cut short by either Adonis's selfishness or Ares's jealousy. That might seem like a romantic idea on the surface, but in the context of this story, Aphrodite has no agency. Her only action is to weep over her dead lover. All myth is metaphor, and there is no version of this story in which Aphrodite isn't positioned as the pitiful keeper of love. The rose quartz carries the complicated legacy of this myth: a goddess portrayed more like a powerless woman, and glorified for her tears.

As a cis person, I was never compelled to consider my gender that deeply. I was told I was a woman and that has always seemed right. But if you ask me why I feel like a woman, I have no answer. I just do. Or do I? Is my womanhood the same as yours? It can't be. My gender is woman, but more specifically, my gender is me.

Other cis women friends of mine say that the only binding quality of womanhood is that it's assigned from the outside, something that's put upon you regardless of how you feel about yourself. Sometimes, this feels correct. My body is seen as womanly and invites the according reactions; the catcalls, the long glares, the ease of close faces and nuzzled necks at sleepovers, the expectation of my presence in nail salons, the shock of a bared nipple, the watching of drinks, the eye contact on public transportation that can only mean *Is this man bothering you? Are you okay?*, the overall awareness of my presence in both positive and negative ways. I am treated as a woman, and that treatment just happens to match what is in my heart.

However, these particular friends have always been perceived as women and have never had to prove their gender. Other women I know, both cis and trans, rage at how quickly that privilege gets taken for granted, the idea that a woman could have something so desperately wanted by others and think of it as a burden. Even as I listed those qualities above, I immediately thought of the woman who has never been comfortable in a circle of girls in a pillowed bedroom, who is deemed too old or too ugly for catcalls, who is not assumed to be a woman at all. There is less and less binding us together all the time. Womanhood is almost everything and almost nothing.

According to much of the Western canon of witchcraft, my womanhood is my power. I have never felt a connection to certain bodily realities of being a cis woman. Menstruation is an annoyance, and thus far pregnancy doesn't interest me. Yet these abilities represent my femininity and are where I'm supposed to derive my craft. It is my "moon-time," my uterus, my hypothetical ability to hold and create life that connects me to the universe in a more powerful way than men. This isn't unique to witchcraft (basically all religions espouse some gender-essentialist idea that "women are sacred . . . in their own way"), and yet for all the sacred power women are said to possess, none of those traditions have landed us in a matriarchy.

Many cultures understand that man and woman are not the only gender identities. In India and Thailand, there are officially recognized third genders, which encompass, to varying degrees, trans, intersex, and nonbinary identities. There are the "Balkan sworn virgins," a socially defined trans masculine role in which, as the *Washington Post* defines it, people assigned female at birth "take an oath of lifelong virginity in exchange for the right to live as men." First Nations groups in the Americas recognize some people as "two spirited." But though there are identities that lie in between, or outside, these categories, they are often still spoken of with language that insists masculinity and femininity are somehow fixed. One and the other, opposites swirling together, both equal and necessary in one person, but still separate. While there are endless gender identities, there are limited-gender roles: man and woman, mother and father, sun and moon, passive and active. A two-dimensional spectrum, a sliding scale between pink and blue, any "third gender" understood as a varying shade of purple between two endpoints.

If femininity doesn't lie in the woman, where is it? The rose quartz promises that the power of love is inherently feminine, and that this feminine nature lives in everyone, but make no mistake, it is not masculine. The language trips me up. I try to talk of gender roles, of gendered expectations and perception and identity, and get looped back into saying men are from Mars and women are from Venus. So much of our world, no matter who you are, is defined and influenced by the relationships, and roles, of men and women. So no, you do not have to be feminine to embrace the energy of a rose quartz, but femininity is a role those perceived as women (whether they are or not) are expected to play. Gender is like money; it's not real, but you still have to use it, or it is used on you.

It's not quite that men and women are punished for acting outside the categories of masculine and feminine—those categories come in many flavors, many combinations we add up and deem correct or deviant. There is a certain kind of femininity that is praiseworthy rather than denigrated in men. It's the kind that views a pink polo shirt as a power move, but keeps pink lipstick at bay. It commends a certain man's soft hands and moisturized face, sometimes, as long as there are other things about him that can counter those qualities so he doesn't tip too far into femininity. But under the right light, some men can grasp at the feminine and stay safe.

Falling in love is possibly the most feminine thing a man can do, by these limited definitions. What is so charming about Ewan McGregor

Gender is
like money;
it's not real,
but you still
have to use
it, or it is
used on you.

as Christian in *Moulin Rouge!* is his utter shock at falling in love. He calls himself a romantic from the get-go, but after meeting Satine, he waves his love around like a hundred-dollar bill he found on the street. Can you believe it? Can you believe this was just here, waiting for me? That I am the keeper of anything this beautiful and soft and nurturing? Of course Satine can believe it; maybe she's been in love before, or has seen men fall for her. It doesn't make her love any less real, just more measured, placed neatly in the context of everything else she's seen. All she has to do, right now, as he's waving his newly found love in her face, is be the recipient, to let him shine his light at her.

But she knows what comes next. She sings of having to eat, of money. She lies to get him a job writing a musical at her club so he can start building his career. She does what's best for him, even if he doesn't understand, even if he gets angry at her, because she loves him. She has to gently take his love, swing it over her shoulders, and carry it for the rest of her life.

▼△▽△

The rose quartz is also the "mothering crystal," representing the relationship we most associate with unconditional love. A mother's unconditional love is seen as necessary—how else could she raise a child who cries and rebels and yells at her and takes her for granted and eventually leaves? To be a good mother, the supposed higher calling of any woman, is to love no matter what. Fathers can love unconditionally as well, but our gender roles tend to give them the job of the disciplinarian, the person whose favor you have to work to win. The giver of unconditional love has only to provide love, and that love has to be given freely and openly and constantly regardless of what she receives in return.

This is reasonable to expect of parents, regardless of gender. But it's also easy to use the act of loving unconditionally as an excuse to treat the woman giving it like shit. The expectations loop back into justifying their existence. Kind, soft, giving: that's just how women are. Any love that comes from a woman is assumed to have the whiff of motherhood in it, whether or not she has or wants children; any person that smacks of the feminine is supposed to be waiting for the smallest opportunity to gush love out of them. Whether you're arguing from witchy empowerment or benevolent misogyny, the conclusion is the same: love is inherently feminine, not just a woman's job, but her nature. Why expect anything else of her if this is what she was made for?

Men are, of course, capable of radiating love's potential and getting no answer, of feeling the sting of unrequited love. But there is often a knot to it. The complaints are made with a hint of entitlement, of expectation that someone should be there to receive their love and be grateful for it, rather than the knowledge that you could spend your whole life ready to accept and return love and die still waiting. When men declare their love, requited or not, it's an intentional gesture. In heterosexual society, women still rarely get the opportunity for the pronouncement, the getting down on one knee to make a moment of their feelings. But love is the pink polo shirt of a man's emotional expression. It's a way to prove one has emotion while still performing the macho posturing of a peacock. It's the grand gesture of the declaration of love, of the proposal.

The romantic ideal of a man in love is only a man in unrequited— or just-about-to-be-requited—love, putting it on display for the world. Once the love becomes mutual, the roles are flipped. Now it's the woman who has to provide love, who has to take that display and nurture it into something they can both live on. The masculine lives in the pursuit, and the feminine is in caring for what you have. The rose quartz's supposed powers may allow a man to get in touch with his feminine nature enough to announce love, but go too far and he becomes feminized, a warped version of the gender roles society creates for us.

I want that challenge. I want to look back at my days of unrequited love and see myself as the hero brave enough to voice my feelings, not the pitiful, pathetic loser assuring myself that if he texted back I'd be so good to him. Sometimes I get a to experience a different gender role—when I present my partner, whose pronouns are they/them/their, with flowers or jewelry for no occasion at all, when they wear lipstick out and I don't, when I make it clear how much I want them, when they cry and I get to be the solid wall they can lean all their weight into. It thrills me, to escape the rose quartz box, even as I remember that none of these actions have any gendered meaning on their own, that this doesn't have to be an issue of jumping over a fence into different, bluer pastures. I don't know that I would have thought these things were opposites if my language didn't present them as such. I don't know I would have thought of the word *opposite* at all.

▼▲▼▲▼

If feminine love is closely tied to motherly love, then it's no wonder that women in heterosexual relationships are sometimes treated by their partners as mother figures, which comes with the expectation that their love be freely and unconditionally given. This is supported by studies that show that women tend to do the lion's share of housework, even if both partners work outside the home.

Women are defined by their ability to love, and their success is often predicated on their relationships with others, including romantic partners and children. A man is lucky to have love, but he isn't defined by whether he has it or not. Bachelors are seen as interesting, sexy, and even mysterious. They can move through the world alone and unencumbered if they choose to. The same cannot be said for spinsters. A woman without love baffles those around her. This expectation hurts women. According to the 2013 study "Commitment: The Key to Women Staying in Abusive Relationships" from researchers at the University of Alabama, "women who consider a relationship with a man as a vital part of their existence as a woman" are less likely to leave an abusive male partner. To hold the gender role of woman is to put the needs of others, including your husband and kids, before your own. A romantic relationship should not be unconditional, and not all are, but all women must confront the reality that they are seen as caretakers.

One of the abilities of the rose quartz, according to *The Book of Stones* by Naisha Ahsian and Robert Simmons, is the ability to heal the heart from past traumas. It can "dissolve one's boundaries of isolation and mistrust," inspire humbleness and humility, and help the user see themselves as one and the same with whoever they are loving. This is love at its best. When your guard is down and the other person sees you and loves you with exactly the same intensity, when whatever work and attention you've put into building this relationship has paid off, then you can roll around in it, still giddy that you're here at all. But I want to know why it's a woman's job to undo her own boundaries. I want to know why her boundaries are thought to be a threat to love instead of a boon to it. I want to know why Satine had to die for Christian to believe she may have been acting out of love the whole time, just not the kind of love he thought he deserved.

The pink color in rose quartz comes from the inclusion of various other elements in a clear quartz—titanium, phosphate, and manganese add anything from a soft pink to a deep rosy color. Some have rutile needles running through them, pink lines cutting through clear stone. It may sound obvious, but the only thing that makes it rose quartz is its color, no matter its internal structure. It's defined solely by its appearance.

Pink used to be a color for baby boys, a bit of trivia trotted out whenever gender reveal parties go awry. According to *Pink and Blue: Telling the Girls from the Boys in America* by Jo B. Paoletti, before the nineteenth century, babies weren't expected to wear gendered clothing at all. White gowns were considered the most convenient and easiest to clean for all children until the age of six. When pastels showed up in the mid-nineteenth century, the baby's coloring, not gender, determined who wore what. By the 1920s, stores like Filene's were suggesting pink for boys and blue for girls, pink being a soft, diluted version of red, the color of Mars, of war, of blood, and blue being the color of the Virgin Mary, of peace and clear skies. But by the 1940s, the colors switched places as clothing manufacturers marketed pink as a color for women and blue as one for men (possibly influenced by the colors of military uniforms). Now, the progressive thing to do is dress them all in yellows and greens, "neutral" colors, though blue has snuck in there too. A baby girl in blue is just a baby. But a baby boy in pink, in frills, in sequins, is cause for confusion.

There are other feminine associations that used to be reserved for men. Greek, Roman, and even Victorian men doused themselves in rose scents. "The rose in times past was a symbol of power, and so of the traditional idea of man," Geza Schoen, a German perfumer, told the *New York Times*'s Rachel Syme in 2016. Though roses have long been associated with Aphrodite and the Virgin Mary, fifteenth-century England's Wars of the Roses was fought between men, carrying white and red roses as the heraldic badges of the House of York and the House of Lancaster. The height of a heel, the grandeur of a wig, the quality of powdered blush were all ways men could one-up each other in court. Things become feminine over time, through association, when the person wearing them is deemed feminine—and less powerful—in their behaviors.

The books and the mystics speak of the rose quartz as if it were always feminine, that its love comes tied with softness and passivity and breasts and puckered lips and motherhood, all valuable and all on one side of an immovable dividing line. But squint and it could have been the stone of men, of Adonis, of boys marching into battle with passion in their hearts, fortified by their childhood pinks. A blue chalcedony could have been the stone of soft, feminine love while rose quartz could have represented the love that leads to acts of bravery, risk, and commitment.

I don't want love to sound like a burden. Being in love, providing love, and receiving love are my favorite things I've ever done. It does not feel like showing up to work or tending a prized orchid to keep love alive. It feels so natural, so inviting, that the ideas of obligation or duty rarely occur to me. Isn't it a joy to be able to express a want or need, and for your partner to say it would be their honor to fulfill it? While any relationship is important to analyze, love is not just work and building and attention. It is magic. Maybe those are the boundaries the rose quartz can help tear down—it can remind you that love should not feel like a job, and when it does, something is wrong.

But that doesn't mean it's unconditional. I asked my partner if there were conditions to their love for me. They said I'd have to force their hand by doing something unthinkably horrible, like murdering their parents. I love them so much sometimes I can't see the boundaries between us. Some days I have to force myself to think of anything but how much I would give, and it feels amazing. But I do know there are actions they could take, however wildly improbable, that would make loving them impossible. Maybe I would still feel something like love for them, but I would stop loving. There are conditions to my love. There are things that would make me abandon it, not because I wanted to, but because I had to. Because the only person I want to have unconditional love for is myself. I think that's what drew me to the rose quartz in the first place.

The most feminine thing about me, in identity and in culture, is that I *love* love. But I can't tell anymore if I give love because I want to or because I have to—because I'm expected and conditioned to, as a woman. Would I love so powerfully if it weren't the "feminine" thing to do? Would I have lost myself in its rosy down if it wasn't expected of me? I still think the greatest thing you'll ever learn is just to love and be loved in return. I just wish it weren't an expectation of the pinker side of the scale.

BLACK TOURMALINE
and Setting
Boundaries

Black Tourmaline

DESCRIPTION:

A semiprecious, iron-rich stone.
Opaque black and shiny, it is brittle
and often fractures unevenly.

COMPOSITION:

Boron silicate

METAPHYSICAL PROPERTIES:

Repels negative energy, whether
from a person or a physical space.
Used to balance and ground nervous
thoughts and keep harmful
people away.

bought my black tourmaline in a panic in 2017. I had been laid off recently, having spent as much time interviewing for the job as I had holding it, and it was the kind of layoff that shook my worldview and made me question every choice I had made. I thought I had done the right thing in seeking a well-paying full-time job and all the stability (and health care) it promised. And now here I was, back to freelancing, scrounging for paychecks and sending desperate follow-up emails to editors "just checking in."

My personal life was also undergoing drastic change. My relationship was moving into a new phase—a good thing, but one that required a lot of talking and emotional energy. My family was reeling from a recent death and a slew of medical emergencies. It seemed like every friend was having a crisis at the same time and was asking me to witness and help. The country was on fire. Nothing else could happen to me, I decided. I couldn't handle it. A few months earlier a friend had gifted me a selenite wand after being told by her tarot reader that no altar was complete without one. Selenite is a crystal known for its healing and soothing energy—a stone of purity, one that bathes everything in warm, clean light and welcomes in the good. But I felt weak when I held it and wished for a moment's peace. I needed something stronger. I didn't need to bring the good in; I needed to keep the bad out.

Black tourmaline is a shield, a bodyguard stone that protects and eliminates negative energy. It's supposed to cleanse you of stress and bad thought patterns, the spiraling negativity and fear that leave you breathless and incapable of action by keeping them from touching you in the first place. But more than that, it supposedly provides protection against negative people, what multiple crystal websites describe verbatim as those "moaners, whiners, complaining neighbors, or emotional vampires who burden you with their problems but do nothing to improve their situations." This is the stone that helps you set boundaries.

I've always thought of my role as the helper, something my partner once described as "assigning myself homework on behalf of other people." Being there for friends, thinking through their problems, and offering solutions, or even just being a shoulder to cry on, is how I tell myself I thrive. But lately I'd been flinching at every text message and Gchat, first from friends who wanted to unload their issues and ask for advice, and then from everyone. I assumed my problem was that I was too giving; I had dropped everything to answer everyone's calls so often, no matter how petty, that I had become a repository for their issues. Focusing on my own needs by sealing myself off seemed necessary, and far easier than being honest about the support I could reasonably

Black tourmaline is a shield, a bodyguard stone that protects and eliminates negative energy.

give or, God forbid, asking my friends for help. It was all very self-pitying: woe is me, the put-upon woman with too many friends!

But as I fingered the selection of half-inch black tourmaline chunks in the back of the crystal store, I told myself the right one would empower me to not respond the second my friends texted, to not plan out two weeks of dinners and parties without a day of rest in between, to not spend my days trying to help everyone else instead of fixing my problems, which I was sure I could do all by myself. In reality, my relationships weren't so one-sided. Of course friends asked me how I was doing, too. But what was I supposed to say other than "fine"? If I wasn't the helper, I was the emotional vampire. If I wasn't giving, I was taking.

▼▲▼▲

Tourmaline comes in all colors of the rainbow, sometimes even a few at once. Because of this, it's often mistaken for other stones. According to the Gem Institute of America, when Spanish colonizers found green and blue gems in Brazil, they sent them home, believing them to be sapphires and emeralds. Dutch colonizers in Sri Lanka did the same, saying they were zircon. Black tourmaline in particular is known as schorl. The German village Zschorlau, nestled in the Saxony Ore mountains, used to be known by this name since the region contained tin mines in which black tourmaline was a common by-product. *Schorl* is also an old mining expression meaning "false ore"; it looks useful, but it's not the thing you actually need. It wasn't until the 1880s that tourmaline (which comes from the Sinhalese for "mixed gems"), in all its color variations, was identified as having its own mineral structure. Black tourmaline was found to be a part of the family.

Black tourmaline is slightly different from its more colorful cousins in that the iron and manganese in its structure make it magnetic, which is probably why words like *grounding* and *shielding* show up so often in descriptions of its metaphysical properties. It can hold a light charge, attract and repel, draw out impurities, and electrocute you if you get near it on a bad day. The color comes from the mineral's ability to absorb what's around it. "Schorls are interesting because tourmalines form in a few stages as they take up whatever is available in the fluid around them," Keiji Hammond, a scientific assistant for mineral deposits at the American Museum of Natural History, told me. "A lot of these tourmalines will just take up so many things until the light doesn't really pass through them and you've got this black coral color." Let's face it, if you're choosing a talisman to protect you against the unwanted, black is a more fitting color than white or pink.

Black tourmaline is thought to be strong, but that's a lie. Black tourmaline is hard but brittle and prone to breaking, leaving a rough, uneven surface. Though the stone has traditionally been used in mourning jewelry, it's not easy to work with. It's too rigid, too unstable to withstand much pressure, and sometimes it can even crumble in your hands. If black tourmaline is the stone of boundaries and protection, it's one whose brittle boundaries are too opaque to see through. It's too weak to be much good at protection at all.

The word *no* has never felt smooth in my mouth. Experiments with it always went awry; someone would start crying, their feelings would be hurt, my parents would make phone calls to the other person's parents to fix things and get us both to apologize, regardless of how measured that *no* might have been. I figured the whole thing wasn't worth it. Instead of learning how and when to say no, I'd find excuses, ways to wrap the *no* in silk so it could slide out of me obscured. Or I wouldn't bother to say anything at all. I never seemed to learn how to do it right, but also, I'm not sure there ever was a way to do it without earning shock or disappointment from someone. If I didn't know how to say no, it's also true that no one else around me learned how to hear it.

Even if I figured out how to say it, I never had any *no*s that were big enough to fight for—no violations of body or privacy or self that the word could have provided a barrier against. All of my unsaid or diluted refusals were over small things, like plans I didn't really want to keep but knew my friend was really looking forward to, or saying yes to takeout burritos when I was craving sushi. It's not just that my *no*s were silent; it's that the stakes always felt too low. There was value, I knew, in going with the flow, or at least in not being the person who repeatedly derailed group plans by insisting everything go her way. I rarely felt, or feel, a hard opinion calcifying inside of me, and in that way it's been easy to be chill and ignore the bigger questions.

I never felt much like I was denying some part of myself in order to stay calm. But my chillness was rewarded, every sign pointing in the direction saying yes, continue going with the flow, there is nothing to even speak up about. I was the "cool girl" who didn't complain, the friend who never caused drama, even if in some fleeting second I wanted to. Letting things happen to me felt so easy, to the point that I never learned the difference between when my needs were being ignored and when I just needed to relax.

For other women, it seems, the temptation to give in to saying no, to be a bitch, is strong, since we're so rarely encouraged to do so. In *You've Got Mail*, Meg Ryan's character, Kathleen Kelly, complains that she is never able to say the exact bit of biting, mean truth the moment she wants to say it and instead is forever victimized by *l'esprit de l'escalier*. Once she meets Tom Hanks's character, Joe Fox (who is secretly her online paramour), she finds that the words come to her immediately, inspired by just what a prick he's being over the crudité. She also finds herself crushed by what she's done. "I was able, for the first time in my life, to say the exact thing I wanted to say at the exact moment I wanted to say it," she writes to Fox, still not knowing he was the one she'd said it to. "And, of course, afterwards, I felt terrible, just as you said I would. I was cruel, and I'm never cruel."

She wasn't cruel. What she said to him—the man who owned the corporate bookstore threatening to put her out of business, who had spent all of their in-person interactions thus far negging her—was that no one would ever remember him, because he is "nothing but a suit." She had no obligation to him, no reason to be polite to him. She didn't know he was her budding soulmate, and he had certainly never treated her as anything but an annoyance. And yet, she felt nothing but guilt.

When I watch that movie now, I think about how I still don't know when and where that obligation exists; the only options seem to be that we're obligated to everyone equally or to no one at all. I think about how when *no* is so forbidden, righteousness can feel like cruelty. I can't decide if Kathleen would have seemed cruel if she knew Joe better— her words certainly would have remained accurate. And I don't know which to trust: the voice that tells me my opinions are valid and should never be tamed for someone else's comfort, or the voice that says, were I to start saying how I really felt, my meanness and indifference would only drive everyone I care about away.

▼▲▼▲

I saw someone tweet about how it felt "empowering" to cancel on a birthday party to stay home and watch a movie. It may have been tongue-in-cheek, but it says something about the modern self-care movement that I couldn't tell whether it was a joke or whether they earnestly thought flaking on a friend was akin to reclaiming some long-lost right. Self-care, boundaries, toxic behavior—it's all easily sloganized and tweetable, and easily used to justify not doing anything you don't feel like doing. Oh, the emotional labor of it all! Doesn't everyone know it's not my job to explain things to them? Don't they know *no* is a complete sentence?

By now, most people understand that when black womanist Audre Lorde said "caring for myself is not self-indulgence, it is self-preservation, and that is an act of political warfare," she was talking about how radical it was to care for her black body and self in a society that doesn't care about black women, and about the need to preserve one's strength and health for an ongoing, collaborative fight against injustice. She was not talking about buying a $30 scented candle and taking a bath because your boss was particularly tedious that day and your boyfriend refuses to vacuum. But when I reach for my black tourmaline, I see all the ways I warp her words to endorse what I think constitutes self-preservation in that moment, when it feels like the world is asking too much of me.

It has been easy for me to find support for saying no, for thinking about my needs instead of the needs of others. Boundaries are in. I'm told by blog posts and thought leaders and anyone with an opinion on "emotional labor" that it is self-care to say no and cut people out of your life, and that you should never be made to justify these actions to anyone. Perhaps it's neoliberalism (or whatever neoliberalism has expanded to mean) seeping into our relationships—friends are assets, interactions should be optimized. Once you've cut out the big problems, start cutting out the little ones until your life is perfect and glistening and as impenetrable as stone.

In a January 2019 piece for BuzzFeed News titled "How Millennials Became the Burnout Generation," writer Anne Helen Petersen makes an argument for how the concept of self-care has become so easy to bastardize. She wrote of the paralysis she has faced when doing "high-effort, low-reward tasks" like getting shoes resoled or making a dermatologist appointment and ascribed the rise of this feeling to a generation that has internalized that their sole value lies in their productivity. "When it came to the mundane, the medium priority, the stuff that wouldn't make my job easier or my work better, I avoided it," she writes. Any problem that arises is something that takes away from work and should be solved so you can get back to work, or takes away from the precious free time you have to relax from work, which you need to not tip fully over into burnout and return to work. After all, you want to be a giver, not a taker, right?

Petersen is a white, cis woman raised middle class; there are plenty of people from more marginalized backgrounds who have been facing this burnout for generations, or who can't afford to give in to exhaustion and unpack what would make their lives fulfilling. But for the privileged, self-care has been divorced from its political origins and has risen as both a cure for and a perpetuator of a culture that values "efficiency" over all else. Meditation, yoga, diets, or anything else Goop has to offer is sold with the implicit goal of having you in top shape so you can perform your best. It's not drastically different from what Lorde spoke of—on its surface the goal is still taking care of yourself so you can be in this for the long haul—only that the work to get back to is typically nothing so crucial as civil rights, and complicated, messy people are more likely to be rejected under the guise that they are "too much work."

When I hold up a black tourmaline shield against a tedious task or a toxic person, I have to ask, why are they toxic? Because they need me at a time that could be better spent working? Because I need to hoard my resources, emotional and otherwise? The language around these emotional shields seems to assume that if we set enough boundaries, we won't have to experience the burden that is other people. Linger too long before the funhouse mirror of self-care, and that's what other people can become: burdens worth investing in only if you can immediately recoup the cost.

Black tourmaline appears in another popular stone: tourmalated quartz. *Quartz* is an umbrella term for a mineral composed of silicon and oxygen; amethyst, agate, onyx, and tiger's-eye all share microstructures—they just differ in color and transparency. But pure, "clear" quartz, on its own, is metaphysically the crystal to end all crystals. It's the conduit through which the spiritual plane supposedly converses, used to elevate consciousness and promote clarity and lift the user out of the funk of everyday life. But black tourmaline punctures through some quartz like needles stuck in ice, scratching through the purity of the clear stone, obscuring its message. This combination can be a good thing, like a healthy dose of skepticism for the perpetually optimistic. Tourmalated quartz is often used to help you stay grounded even as you reach for the newer and better. But it's reminiscent of the way paranoia seeps into honest thought. We may know, somewhere, what self-care looks like, but it's clouded by self-indulgence.

The language around these emotional shields seems to assume that if we set enough boundaries, we won't have to experience the burden that is other people. Linger too long before the fun-house mirror of self-care, and that's what other people can become: burdens, only worth investing in if you can immediately recoup the cost.

It's easier to cut everyone out than to learn to differentiate between the chronically demanding and the occasionally needy. It's war, we convince ourselves; there is no middle ground when people come for your precious energy, which is already spread so thin. It's kill or be killed.

▽▲▽▲

When I was sixteen, an elder threatened to cut me out of their life. I had lied to them. I was angry over something they had done but didn't know how to say so to someone who had power over me. So I broke something of theirs in a fit of frustration and passed it off as an accident. They told me they had no place for liars in their life and that if I was lying I could get out. They made it seem so easy. It hadn't taken a history of abuse for them to cut me off, or at least threaten to. One teenage lie, stemming from one moment of justifiable anger, was enough. I don't know if this was the root of my paranoia (I've always been a people pleaser), but I've found myself unable to figure out what's self-care and what isn't. The threat of hurting or losing others by setting boundaries is always there.

Another lifetime later, I canceled on a friend's birthday party and cried myself to sleep. I was feeling sick, likely because of some questionable cheese sauce served with a warm pretzel the night before. Before that, fantasies of canceling had skipped through my mind—the party was over an hour away on a crumbling subway, on a night that looked like rain, at the end of a week of feeling uncomfortable in my own body for this reason or that. My partner looked at me with pity as I pawed through my sweaters, every few seconds gasping and grimacing with gas pain. "You're sick! We can stay home, it's fine," they begged as my eyes started to water and I threw myself onto the bed.

It should not have been such a dramatic decision to make, but I couldn't stop crying. For nearly three hours, after we had agreed not to go and after I changed into sweatpants and after we turned on a movie, tears streamed down my face. I texted my friends I was sorry, and they wished me well and said everything was fine, and I wailed like someone had died. My partner became increasingly stunned; this was not a logical reaction, but logic was no help. They reminded me our friends were not mad at me, but I didn't believe it. They asked me if I'd be mad if the tables were turned, but they didn't understand. In my anxiety and paranoia, I had decided that this was it—the moment that everyone learned I was a selfish flake and decided once and for all that I wasn't worth loving anymore.

If you're taught that self-care or saying no is inherently selfish, it becomes harder to tell what's actually selfish. But whereas the black tourmaline may give you the strength to block out toxic people and experiences, it doesn't give you the wisdom to know what to block, and when, nor does it let you see your own needs clearly. When I turn off Gchat and Slack and don't answer my text messages, I might think I'm justified, but a voice reminds me that other people might not be there waiting when I return. Protecting my boundaries, even if I need them in the moment, might result in other walls being thrown up against me. And that threat makes every inconvenience seem like the end.

We all know emotional leeches. They are the people who never ask about anyone but themselves, who demand your time and attention, and who guilt you when you can't give them and yet never offer theirs. But sometimes, we all need to leech. We've all needed a friend in the middle of the night, or for longer stretches of time than we'd like. We've all been so enveloped in our own grief or pain or depression that we forget to check in on those we care about. We've all asked those we love to schlep in bad weather to our birthday parties. It's not even leeching. We all ask things of each other.

I probably could use a shield. I could stand to say no more often, to not feel the need to justify why I'm not interested in a certain trip or activity or even conversation. I could stand to not be undone by admitting I'm too sick to go to a birthday party, because the people I'd say that to are not emotional leeches, nor do they think of me as such. These are people who love me, who have dropped everything to help me before, who have demonstrated time and again that they are there for me. And yet, even with them, I am held back from total honesty by the learned fear of being a bitch. What if that one *no* is all it takes for all my support structures to come crashing down—for everyone else to believe I'm the leech they no longer have time for?

This mentality is the toxic thing, as well as the assumption that everything is happening to me, on purpose—that it's me against the world and not me within it. The way forward is to accept my missteps, to honor them, so that I can extend that same grace to others. It is only on the rarest occasions that a shield is what helps.

I think of self-care as a way to recoup my energy so I can keep giving it to others. I don't want my relationships to be transactional. I still don't know where *no* fits in. I haven't yet gained the wisdom to know when self-care looks like setting boundaries and when it looks like going with the flow, even if I would have done things differently. Until I figure it out, I'll use my black tourmaline with caution, and often with a positive, light-bringing stone like selenite or quartz. There's no use in keeping the bad out if you can't be vulnerable enough to let good things in.

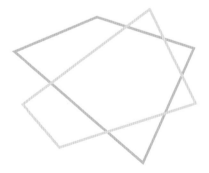

PEARL
and the
White Light of
Innocence

Pearl

DESCRIPTION:

An iridescent mineral made within
the soft tissue of a shelled mollusk,
but still prized as a gemstone

COMPOSITION:

Calcium carbonate

METAPHYSICAL PROPERTIES:

A stone of purity and innocence.
It is said to soothe negative energy
and bring balance and wisdom
to one's actions.

During my freshman year of college, I experienced deep horror upon learning that the girl across the hall wore her pearls to the gym. She fancied herself a Massachusetts prep, all seersucker and boat shoes and high ponytails. I'd see her returning red-faced from the treadmill, her strand of pearls slicked in sweat. When we'd go out, I'd see her spritz Clinique Happy onto her pearl-studded neck, and then come home and pass out drunk after partying in the Louisiana humidity without bothering to take the necklace off and put it back in its velvet box. Something so delicate seemed out of place for the life we were living at eighteen.

According to *The Official Preppy Handbook*, the 1980 humor book edited by Lisa Birnbach, pearls are an integral part of the uniform for any preppy woman. For a debut ball "you will need white kid gloves, white shoes and pearls." After one's debut, "prep women never take off their jewelry—pearls on the squash court are perfectly acceptable." And even if you're not sporting a modest strand around your neck, studs in your ears are acceptable for all occasions. Birnbach extended that ubiquity to nudity in a 2016 article for *Town and Country*, writing that even when the true prep is naked on her honeymoon, she should still be wearing her pearl studs and her engagement ring.

Whenever my hallmate would return from the gym, I'd cringe with both worry and smug self-satisfaction. My grandmother, prep that she was, taught me that pearls are finicky. They fade with sweat but need body oil to maintain their luster. They don't respond well to perfume, cosmetics, or arid climates. They're scratched easily by other sharp gems and shouldn't come in contact with direct sunlight, high temperatures, vinegar, laundry detergent, or fruit juice.

The squash court seems like a horrible place for them. Pearls are innocent and must be protected.

A pearl is nurtured by the organism it's born into, lacquered and polished into its full beauty, and if it weren't for us, it would never leave its home. This complicates things, metaphysically speaking. "Since the oyster must be killed to remove the pearl, some believe there is a heavy debt incurred by those who engage in trafficking pearls and by those who wear and use them," writes author Scott Cunningham in *Cunningham's Encyclopedia of Crystal, Gem & Metal Magic*. There is violence inherent in their stories, whether it's the Japanese myth that pearls are the tears of mermaids or the Greek belief that pearls could keep a new bride from crying (because of course she would cry). "Popular folklore naming pearls as bearers of bad luck might be connected with the violence of their collection. You'll know intuitively whether you can use them or not."

A pearl is nurtured by the organism it's born into, lacquered and polished into its full beauty, and if it weren't for us, it would never leave its home.

If a pearl is a reminder of innocence and purity, it is also a reminder that there is no innocence without the possibility of its loss, no purity without the impure. If the pearl is a symbol of innocence, it is only because we know what decay looks like. No matter how well you treat it, something can only stay pure for so long. Its end is as inevitable as the violence that will cause it.

▼▲▼▲▼

Pearls sometimes seem like more hassle than they're worth. Even before we knew how they were formed, pearls inspired the language of cautious magic. "The quality of the pearl depends much more upon a calm state of the heavens than of the sea," wrote Pliny the Elder in *Natural History*, "and hence it is that it contracts a cloudy hue, or a limpid appearance, according to the degree of serenity of the sky in the morning."

The pearl is a result of an itch, its nacre coating the result of a compulsive healing behavior, like licking a wound. Natural pearls are formed when a piece of sand or grit finds its way into an oyster, whereas cultured pearls are born of the farmer placing the irritant inside. Pearls sit like pimples on the mollusk's gooey, slick flesh. A smattering of iridescent zits. Once they're removed from their corporeal incubators, their appeal is undeniable. The pearl itself is a symbol of honesty, purity, and protection. It has magical associations with the moon and water, based on where it comes from, and is said to have a sedative effect, as if the magician herself has been gently rocked and covered in a protective gloss. Saint Hildegard believed they had the power to purify water, perhaps as an extension of what oysters do as filter feeders. But as symbols of purity and truth, of refinement and sincerity, you could do worse than a luminous bead plucked from the flesh of the sea.

There are almost no myths that evoke innocence and purity without young women. In Hindu myth, the god Krishna picked the first pearls from the ocean and presented them to his daughter on her wedding day;

pearls are still a part of many Hindu weddings, whether as bridal accessories or offerings to gods. They were presented by ladies to knights to wear at tournaments in medieval Europe. The traditionally female name Margarita (and all derivatives) come from the Greek word for pearl, of which there is no male equivalent. In Chinese medicine, only "virgin" pearls were used in healing, not those that had been bored for jewelry—which is extremely A Metaphor. The implication is women, like pearls, are worth the most (to men, to society) when they are young and untouched. "Unlike other gems, a pearl comes to us perfect and beautiful, direct from the hand of nature," writes mineralogist George Kunz in *The Book of the Pearl*. The pearl owes nothing to humans, "and there is a purity and sweetness about it which makes it especially suitable for the maiden."

Pearl is an embarrassingly allegorical name for a child of sin, but then again, Nathaniel Hawthorne's 1850 novel *The Scarlet Letter* is an embarrassingly allegorical book. Hester Prynne's daughter Pearl, the result of Hester's infidelity, is a wild and witchy child, though the Puritan community blames that on her mother's deeds and not on the fact that they shunned her and made her live on the edge of town. It's no surprise she has little interest in the society that condemns her existence. In "Hawthorne's Pearl: Woman-Child of the Future," published in 2005 in *American Transcendental Quarterly*, Cindy Lou Daniels writes that the child "is neither forced into displaying guilt, nor into hiding it, because she does not own the guilt brought into her life by her mother and her mother's lover."

Hester uses Pearl to thwart that guilt by dressing her in elaborate, beautiful things that serve two purposes: signaling to outsiders that Pearl is good and worthy, and reminding Hester herself that something beautiful has come out of her "shameful" act. Another easy metaphor to make with pearls is birth. They are beautiful, delicate objects created by a living creature, ripped from those bodies, and then used by outsiders in the way their creators could never imagine. Mother-of-pearl is the name given to the iridescent inner layer of the mollusks that also makes up the outer layer of pearls, a protective coating passed from parent to child in the hopes it will be enough. Pearls are harvested and pierced and worn to the gym regardless. It is not enough.

Hawthorne tries to argue that Hester's sartorial efforts were in vain. "So magnificent was the small figure, when thus arrayed, and such was the splendor of Pearl's own beauty, shining through the gorgeous robes which might have extinguished a paler loveliness, that there was an absolute circle of radiance around her, on the darksome cottage floor," he wrote. "And yet a russet gown, torn and soiled with the child's rude play, made a picture of her just as perfect." She would have been beautiful no matter what, he tries to say. Except that's not quite right. Though the Puritans were skeptical of Pearl either way, the clothes helped; that she was obviously beautiful even in a torn dress made them madder. Her mother's protective layers allowed her to have at least the appearance of civility, like she was one of them, to let the Puritans forget, just for a moment, that her provenance had no effect on the beauty God had bestowed on her, and that she is as good as any of them despite the supposed sin at her core.

It's rare that someone would look at a pearl and think of the dirt at the center. If they do, it would be more to marvel than to disparage. But then again, that's sort of the draw of the pearl—something beautiful and dirty at once, something that has to be stolen from a disgusting place and can never be looked at without remembering just how and why it came to be. In *Natural History*, Pliny the Elder writes of how difficult pearls are to harvest. "The fish, as soon as ever it perceives the hand, shuts its shell and covers up its treasures, being well aware that it is for them that it is sought; and if it happens to catch the hand, it cuts it off with the sharp edge of the shell. And no punishment is there that could be more justly inflicted." If you could risk losing your hand, you'd think you might make do with a quartz found in the dirt. But I'm sure there's some idiom about risk and reward that anyone who has ever dived for pearls has told themselves.

In a 1997 episode of *The Simpsons* called "Homer's Phobia," the gay antiques dealer John (voiced by John Waters) is delighted at the retro camp of the Simpsons' home. Marge serves Hi-C and fluffernutters. There's corn on the kitchen curtains. And, he coos at Lisa, "pearls on a little girl. It's a fairy tale!" There is no deeper metaphor to his delight. Pearls are sweet and innocent and almost campily so, like a Pat Boone record, like a little girl should be.

I feel old in pearls. My main association with them is accompanying my grandfather on Christmas Eve to buy my grandmother a new strand. He always did his shopping on Christmas Eve; the store clerks really turned on the charm (and sometimes passed out free food and eggnog) the last few hours before the jewelry shop closed. We brought her old strand to make sure we didn't accidentally buy two of the same size, and my grandpa draped them both on my thirteen-year-old neck to compare. They were beautiful, and I figured someday I'd be elegant and refined enough to merit them. This was a necklace for an old-fashioned kind of girl intent on growing into an old-fashioned kind of woman, not for the girl I was. But maybe someday.

I stayed naive for a long time. My friends were the kind of girls who were always sneaking new, dirty things into our lives, the kind of girls who'd make up sexy dances to the *Miss Saigon* soundtrack, call me a "pussy" for crying at scary movies, and stuff their bras with tissues. The kind of girls who'd get fingered on a group date to the movies while I sat four seats down, still waiting for my first kiss. I was considered the innocent one among my friends, the good one, the one that needed protection. But eventually, though it took longer than I wanted, the spell of innocence started to lift. By the time I went with my grandpa to buy the necklace, whatever I had learned of sex and heartbreak and the savviness required to navigate my city (which, to be fair, wasn't much) seemed enough that the label of innocent should no longer apply to me. I had begun to want things—the freedom to go out with my friends, the pleasure that came from touching my body, the thrill of romantic pursuit. I had learned, somewhere, that the presence of these feelings meant innocence could no longer thrive, something I could only sense as soon as I didn't have it. But I didn't understand why I should want it, or why the lack of it should make me feel somehow guilty. If the information I was absorbing about the world every minute was useful, why was it treated like a shame?

According to one myth, white pearls come from the tears of Eve, and black pearls from the tears of Adam, sobbing as they were cast out of Eden. Perhaps they are the last bits of innocence leaving their bodies. Religious interpretations aside, there's a reason Eve's story is compelling. By the time she bites the fruit it no longer matters whether she's innocent or not. It's her desire that blows the garden open.

The joke about debutantes is that the traditional white dress and kid gloves are rarely appropriate by the time these young women make their debut, but debs can pass better than most. Innocence depends as much on what we think it looks like as it does on actual behavior and knowledge. That metaphorical veil gives you the benefit of the doubt. There are many forms that veil can take. The white, well-off girls (they were all white, and we all lived on the Upper East Side) getting fingered at the movie theater would not be doomed by their behavior, through some combination of their whiteness and richness and other cultural signifiers. They could still call on the protection of childhood if they wanted. Yet multiple studies confirm that black children are routinely perceived as older than their white peers, and more likely to be viewed as guilty when suspected of a crime or even just transgressive behavior. In a 2017 study from the Georgetown Law Center, in which adults (mostly white women) were surveyed about girlhood, "black girls were more likely to be viewed as behaving and seeming older than their stated age," starting from the age of five. Participants in the study "perceived black girls as needing less protection and nurturing than white girls, and that black girls were perceived to know more about adult topics and are more knowledgeable about sex than their white peers."

Some girls get to wear innocence longer than others, whether because of race or class or affect. But other girls, usually from marginalized backgrounds, are sexualized in spite of their childhood, or sexualized for it—different flavors of rotten fruit from the same tree. Elvis Presley famously favored white, cotton panties on all the white teen girls he lured into bed. It is overwhelmingly white girls who are fetishized for their Catholic school uniforms, or for being "barely legal," or for inspiring men to set internet countdown clocks to the day they turn eighteen. Meanwhile, teenage Aaliyah was considered mature enough to be in a relationship with R. Kelly. Maybe my college hallmate knew better than I did what pearls at the gym signified. They were meant to protect her—which is why it didn't matter if she protected them. If she ruined them with her sweat, she could just buy another strand.

"Invoking the image of innocent and pure white women in constant need of protection, the men endeavored to perform their manly duties as fathers, husbands, and brothers," wrote Crystal Nicole Feimster in the 2011 book *Southern Horrors: Women and the Politics of Rape and Lynching*, describing the lynching of Ephraim and Henry Grizzard in 1892. The brothers were accused of raping Mollie and Sadie Bruce, two young white women who lived just outside Nashville. A group of "deputized citizens" found Henry first, and after the Bruce sisters identified him as one of their assailants, he was turned over to the lynch mob by the sheriff. But, Feimster writes, "the lunchtime lynching failed to satisfy the mob's taste for revenge," and the mob took Ephraim from the jail where he was being held, injuring a number of officers in the process, and hanged him too. The headline in the *Indianapolis Journal* read "grizzard lynched at last" and did not mention the Bruce sisters.

Some of the most unforgivable violence has been committed in the name of protecting innocence personified. Women and children—especially of the dominant race or higher class—are victims of the benevolent misogyny that both lumps them together and insists they are inherently pure in a way adult men are not. It is a justification for men's actions toward them and in their name. *Women are pure, we have to protect them* grows from the same roots as *Men are evil, we must harm.*

Women have also taken up the mantle of purity to maintain their conditional privileges. In the 1910s, Josephine Dodge, cofounder of the National Association Opposed to Women's Suffrage, argued against giving women the right to vote in the United States. "The life of the average woman is not so ordered as to give her firsthand knowledge of those things which are the essentials of sound government," she said at one meeting in New Jersey. "She is worthily employed in other departments of life, and the vote will not help her fulfill her obligations therein." Better not to sully herself with dirty politics. Better to stay in the home and wield her power there, where she can influence her husband's vote in subtler ways.

Many suffragists, conversely, assumed that women's "inherent" purity would improve political discourse. But anarchist Emma Goldman was skeptical of the power of the women's vote. This was mostly because she knew true revolution would never be on a ballot and that women were deluded in their assumption that their purity would make politics better. "Woman will purify politics, we are assured. . . . To assume, therefore, that she would succeed in purifying something which is not susceptible of purification, is to credit her with supernatural powers," she wrote in her essay "Woman Suffrage," which was included in her 1910 work *Anarchism and Other Essays.* In fact, she argues that women's purist attitudes, though they may be socially inherited, make them a greater liability in the political realm, essentially busybodies hell-bent on regulating drink, prostitution, and gambling instead of fighting for equality. "Man has long overcome the superstitions that still engulf woman. . . . He therefore had neither time nor inclination to measure everyone's morality with a Puritanic yardstick."

It is only women (usually white) who clutch their pearls, both because they have been conditioned to and because they have accepted those conditions as fair compensation for their protection. Their perceived innocence is all they have. But I do not know the value of innocence except as a false barrier to predators, something considered, absorbed, and then discarded by the wrong kind of beholder. To them, innocence invites dirt; it's a blank canvas asking to be smeared, begging for the color of experience. It's an invitation for predatory behavior.

The Nashville mob wanted to show Ephraim Grizzard's body to the white women in what Feimster says was both a display of their imagined bravery and a "form of terror." *Look what your innocence made me do.*

▼▲▼▲

The most famous shell-based birth is that of Venus, of whom the pearl is one of many symbols. The Roman goddess was born of the ocean, supposedly after Saturn castrated his father, Uranus, and his blood fell into the sea; a radiant good from a dark sin. The scene was set in a Homeric hymn:

> *Of august gold-wreathed and beautiful*
> *Aphrodite I shall sing to whose domain*
> *belong the battlements of all sea-loved*
> *Cyprus where, blown by the moist breath*
> *of Zephyros, she was carried over the*
> *waves of the resounding sea on soft foam.*

Venus is a dynamic goddess. She represents sex and fertility, growth and renewal, beauty and love, and the victory that comes when those things are yours. But she also represents the opposite of sexuality and fertility: chastity. "Venus Verticordia" was the changer of hearts and had the ability to turn the sexual vice in her followers into virtue. She inspired maidens to stay chaste and married women to stay true to their husbands, even when temptation called. For all her championing of sex and baby-making, these had to happen within the prescribed confines of patriarchal society. The heart should only change one way.

In Venus's most famous visual depiction, by Botticelli, she is demure even on her the day of her birth, covering her vulva and one breast, her shy contrapposto reminding you she is nude but not naked. If you want her, that's because of your own projections. But the story isn't always told this way. In some images, the goddess is standing, arms outstretched, in the middle of the shell. In *Birth of Venus* by Alexandre Cabanel, she is lying naked on top of the foam, her hair mingling with the waves, as cherubs announce her to the world. In one painting by Henri Pierre Picou, she is nestled in a shell the length of her body, luxuriating in her bed alone, more woman than goddess. If she can turn your heart toward chastity, she is also there to remind you what you are turning away from.

▼▲▼▲▼▲

In 1929, the *New York Times*'s Herbert L. Matthews painted at once a harsh and romantic picture of Mikimoto Kōkichi and his pearl farm. Mikimoto had been experimenting since the 1880s with creating a perfectly spherical cultured pearl, a pearl made by intentionally seeding an oyster with a sphere of mother-of-pearl, rather than opening as many wild oysters as possible and hoping to find matching stones. By the 1920s he had made the process commercially viable. His pearls completely upended the industry, which until then had been based mainly in Paris and relied on nature to do all the work of creation. Matthews writes of Mikimoto's farm on the Gokasho Bay, where "thousands upon thousands of oysters are patiently working night and day like so many obedient slaves, doing the bidding of their lord and master." The pearls were harvested by women, who were deemed better divers than men and who wore nothing but a "flimsy white cotton garment" to protect them from the cold of the water. "They are splendid specimens of femininity," wrote Matthews, "all of them."

It's a beautiful inversion of the Western metaphors of violence and purity—this time the pearls are being rescued from the "slaves" not by brute male force, but by the kindred, gentle spirit of a woman in white. Matthews referred to them as "girls," implying youth and virginity, and sex by extension. The "honor" the lynch mobs were protecting was always that of the imagined white hymen. If pearls are worn by proper, virtuous, and refined women, it's because they suggest those women's innocence is directly tied to sex.

Virginity always comes with a limited time frame. Miss Havisham sitting in her wedding dress as her mansion crumbles around her is an unnatural sight, too old now to be wearing white lace and ignorant of bodily pleasures (we assume). Steve Carrell's forty-year-old virgin inspires a multipronged crusade by his friends, who are clearly uncomfortable by his mere presence, in order to get him laid. Too much innocence turns into its own kind of vulgarity, and even those who are allowed to be innocent have to give it up eventually. It's only worth something if it's ephemeral.

"Human beings have no monopoly on physical virginity," wrote Hanne Blank in her 2007 book *Virginity: The Untouched History*. "But we have cornered the market on it, both in terms of recognizing that it exists and in making it useful in the way we organize our cultures and our relationships with one another." We socially regulate who should be having sex, with whom, when, and how (cis men and women, when they get married, and in a way that will produce children, respectively). In modern society, few people order their sexual lives around such strict mores, but those ideas have informed Western values around sex.

Blank outlines the anthropological developments that led to our modern ideas of virginity and virtue: the rise of agriculture, the concept of individual ownership, the importance of the right of primogeniture in property transfers, and the economic value of a virginal daughter and the dowry she could attract. Virginity has no inherent value, but it has been economically and morally encoded into society's perception of a woman's worth.

Whether or not money is involved, a woman's virginity is still insidiously considered to have worth. The idea that a woman who has never had sex is more desirable on some level than a woman who knows what she is doing is a well-worn punchline in sitcoms and teen comedies. It's in *Cruel Intentions*, in which Sebastian, a rich playboy, initially sees his vampy, sexually liberated ex-stepsister Kathryn as the prize until blonde, virginal Annette entices him with her purity, thereby purifying him. It's in *Fifty Shades of Grey*, in which Christian repeatedly implies that Anastasia's innocence has drawn him to her. The fact that she's a virgin makes him all the hornier. It's also embedded in every joke about a dad meeting his daughter's prom date on the front porch with a shotgun.

For all the desire expressed, the act of losing one's virginity is framed as just that—a loss. You do not gain sexual knowledge, but rather something is taken from you. No other rites of passage are described in this way. I have trained myself to tell the story of "the first time I had sex" instead of "the time I lost my virginity," though the hard pause I give before uttering the phrase is a dead giveaway that this language doesn't come naturally to me. As problematic as the word *virginity* can be, at least its succinct; I still haven't been able to force out "the first time I had penetrative sex with someone with a penis."

When I was seventeen, I called an ex and asked if they wanted to have sex. I was heading to college, which I viewed first and foremost as a place for hooking up without worrying about running into your parents. I refused to leave high school without knowing what I was doing, so I presented what I thought was a reasonable proposition: we're still friends, we're still comfortable with each other, let's get this sex thing out of the way so it's not such a daunting prospect. I do not remember the sex. What I remember is the train ride to my ex's college, watching cartoons in a dorm room and waiting until it was nighttime (because this is the sort of thing that should be done at night). I remember my chilled skin against a polyfil comforter. I remember laughing when the geometry of our bodies didn't line up correctly, and then the surprise when it did. Afterward, we laid cramped in the twin bed together, feeling like we had a secret and thinking I wouldn't want it any other way. I didn't feel anything like loss.

When I told a future boyfriend about this, he was baffled that I had no regrets and insisted I was somehow wrong in the way I handled it. To him, my experience was sullied by my explicit orchestrations; it should have just . . . happened. The idea of virginity as moral gift had a firm grip on his psyche, which would cause problems later, but at the time I listened patiently as he told me this moment in my life was worth less because it hadn't happened "naturally."

A pearl is just an oyster's shining scab, and a hymen is just something your body made. There is nothing moral or pure about either, and there's nothing natural about the energy it takes to maintain innocence. His confusion didn't make me regret my choice, but the knowledge that my peers could still care so deeply about the "right" way to reach such a milestone slipped into me like a splinter. Even after we've grown up, an aura of purity is still something we're willing to invest in both protecting and projecting.

Before we cultured them in long rows, pearls were always a discovery. You could crack open a hundred oysters and leave their flesh to rot on the rocks without finding a single one, or you could open shell after shell filled with precious wounds. The not knowing is the thrill.

But by the time you're standing there on your wedding night, ring on your finger and pearls on your neck, you know. I think it's as simple as longing. Innocence is potential. It is a moon-like cloak pulled over the implied vulgarity of reality, the hope that something pure can survive, and even thrive, surrounded by unspeakable things. A strand of pearls on a debutante is visual semantics we still value. A strand of pearls says, *There's still a part of me you can't know. I'm too delicate to show you but there's something filthy at the center of me. Doesn't that make you want me more?*

PYRITE,
Impostors,
and
Fools

Pyrite

DESCRIPTION:

A metallic mineral ranging
from silver to brassy gold in color,
which often naturally forms cubes

COMPOSITION:

Iron sulfide (FeS_2)

METAPHYSICAL PROPERTIES:

A stone of luck and encouragement
that helps release negative behavior
patterns and promote inspiration.
Keeping a pyrite in your workspace
is said to help dispel intellectual fatigue.

Mary-Kate and Ashley Olsen briefly sold me on "pyrite baron" as a future career. In their 1994 TV movie *How the West Was Fun*, which I owned, along with many other Dualstar productions, on VHS, the twins are called to their godmother's dude ranch in the American West. The ranch is losing money and she's keen on selling, so the girls get their dad fired from his job (a thing that, apparently, daughters can do) and head out to help, in the way these films assumed only nine-year-olds could.

At the ranch, they meet the son of the ranch hand and Scooby Doo–type villain, Bart, who has been intentionally turning people away from the business and has plans to sell it and convert it into a gaudy theme park. The girls, as always, have a plan and invite investors (again, nine-year-olds can do this?) to see how wonderful the ranch could be on its own, without roller coasters and cotton candy booths. But on the day the investors come to visit, the sisters' vision for an enthralling tour of the ranch is thwarted by Bart at every turn. The girls' last shot to convince the investors to save the ranch is to follow a mysterious map that promises golden treasure at the end of the path.

Where X marks the spot, they discover a cave full of sparkling gold embedded in the rock. For a moment, the girls think the ranch is saved, with or without the suits' money. Except the cave isn't full of gold. It's pyrite, an iron sulfide with a pale, brassy color that tricked many ignorant prospectors at the height of the gold rush and is functionally worthless. The Olsen twins' plans are foiled again. But when the girls think all hope is lost, the investors burst into applause. It might just be iron sulfide, but the whole thrilling horseback adventure to finding the shining cave is an experience they can sell. Who cares if the gold isn't real? Or the adventure, for that matter? It feels enough like the real thing to be fun, and at that point, what's the difference? The potential fortune is the same.

I have two pyrites. One is a nearly perfect yellowed cube, with striations that look like a moonscape in miniature, or like that one Joy Division album cover. (You know the one.) The second is newly tumbled and smooth on its surface, with open maws revealing the ore's geometric crags reflecting each other into the void. They sometimes look like gold, if you squint, but mostly they look like metallic earth. Pyrite was once my favorite mineral in my small childhood collection, my specimen of which came glued to a sheet of paper from some museum store. It seemed obviously more beautiful than the other stones, bright and bold where others were dull and translucent, like it knew exactly what it was. And yet there was its nickname, fool's gold, quoted just beneath it on the paper grid. At some point the name registered, and I began to feel like a fool for loving it so. Gold was the thing I should be obsessed with, not this lowly imitator.

Pyrite got the name fool's gold when California prospectors would think they had found their fortune sifting through a muddy pool, only to realize the glinting shard wasn't the kind of metal that would make them rich. It was commonly defined by what it wasn't—not gold, not valuable, not worthy. No one cared that investment in pyrite ore, which is used to make sulfuric acid, would quickly become a smarter investment than gold, as America scrambled to ditch foreign imports during World War I. No one cared that the presence of pyrite in soil often meant that real gold was not far away. It was only what it couldn't be.

◣◢◣◢

Impostor syndrome was first recorded in 1978 in a study by doctors Pauline Rose Clance and Suzanne Imes, although they referred to it as "impostor phenomenon." They described it as "the psychological experience of believing that one's accomplishments came about not through genuine ability, but as a result of having been lucky, having worked harder than others, or having manipulated other people's impressions." The doctors first observed the phenomenon in women; indeed, the study was inspired by Clance's own feelings of inferiority in her graduate studies. However, later studies showed that people of other genders are prone to the same feelings of anxiety around their success, as if they're pulling one over on everyone they know, and that any achievement is a blip of luck that could never be replicated.

In a 1993 report on impostor phenomenon, Clance and another doctor, Joe Langford, compiled several surveys conducted in the intervening years that looked at the reactions among (presumably cis) men and women to the idea that one doesn't deserve to be in the room, and they found it equally prevalent among men and women. Rather than viewing the pursuit of intelligence or success as a never-ending journey, men and women who experienced impostor phenomenon viewed these experiences as objective peaks that they would never be able to scale.

What was different, however, was how that feeling manifested outwardly. "For females, impostor feelings had low correlations with impulsivity and need for change, consistent with the usual description of impostors as cautious and unlikely to engage in risk-taking," wrote Clance and Langford, but men "tend to compensate by pushing themselves in a frenetic manner in order to prove their competency." In other words, women tend to shy away from the spotlight when they feel like they don't belong, afraid too much attention will expose them as the fakes they are. Men bulldoze ahead, convinced that bombast will make up for shortcomings in the quality of their work. Give 'em the ol' razzle-dazzle.

Both tendencies focus on the disconnect between appearance and reality; the fear is that being seen as competent doesn't matter if you know your work isn't up to par. But the reverse is also true for many sufferers of impostor syndrome—that your work can be as good as anyone else's but it won't matter if you're seen as a fraud. You can be stronger than gold, more useful than gold, more valuable, but if gold is what they're looking for, you'll never be enough. When I feel like everyone can see right through me and that nothing I do will ever be enough, I wonder if there's a cure for feeling like this. Therapy is certainly helpful, but it's not a cure-all. In Clance and Imes's original study, they singled out "having worked harder than others" as one reason someone might believe they had not achieved their success through genuine ability, as if working hard to achieve something isn't the definition of genuine ability. Maybe a person thinks she's a fraud because she worked hard rather than having it come "naturally" to her, that the difficulty of the task belies some inherent incompetence. But maybe she's right. Maybe in a vacuum she wouldn't have that talent. Maybe her hard work was bolstered by privilege and selective opportunity available to her and not others, and that should add a footnote to her work.

It'd be easy to look at all of these examples of impostor syndrome and conclude that any time someone feels like an impostor, it's false. She must have been kicking ass and just been made to feel inferior by her boss or her boyfriend or racism or, like, society. And who gets to determine who's an impostor anyway? Whose perspective are we trying to live up to? I wouldn't be surprised if the women in those studies had some phantom man's voice in their head (perhaps disguised as their own) telling them their success was undeserved and their competence was just the result of their peers taking pity on them.

But the cultural acknowledgment of impostor syndrome sidesteps instances in which someone *is* an impostor, or when someone correctly assesses their abilities. I think of how Elizabeth Holmes may have benefitted from a little self-doubt while running Theranos. I think of how we need more men to have the self-awareness so many women are expected to possess, rather than having more women careening forward, fueled only by unearned confidence. Leaning in works only when you know your work is being undervalued, not when everyone has made an accurate assessment of you and you just need more time to percolate.

In 2015, comedian Jessica Williams received blowback when she said she had no interest in, and wasn't ready to, host *The Daily Show* after Jon Stewart stepped down. "Thank you but I am extremely underqualified for the job!" she tweeted in response to hundreds of suggestions that she would be a perfect fit. "At this age (25) if something happens politically that I don't agree with, I need to go to my room & like not come out for, like, 7 days." It was a statement that showed maturity and self-possession; just because a bunch of people said she was ready to lead one of America's most popular talk shows, one that had shaped politics for over a decade, doesn't mean that she was.

Her fans wouldn't have it. There was a petition calling her a "genius" and "natural successor" to Stewart, and an article in the *Billfold* theorized that she was a victim of impostor syndrome and that all she needed was a good pep talk. Author Ester Bloom imagined a room of "old white people" congratulating themselves on Williams's statement.

"We did it, they whisper. We have succeeded in instilling in yet another competent, confident young woman a total lack of understanding of her own self-worth!" Williams responded to the article in harsher terms, and in particular to the implication that a white woman knew better than a black woman what was good for her. "Are you unaware how insulting that can be for a fully functioning person to hear that her choices are invalid?" Williams wrote. "Is it possible that I know & love myself enough to admit what I'm not ready for?"

Of course it is possible. But the paranoia behind impostor syndrome, of being the fool's version of our best selves, is: how do we know we know? Our fears may seem grounded and reasonable, but they could just be a trick. On the other hand, our confidence could be built on nothing.

On some level, I can't accept praise. Every time I feel like I've earned something, I also feel like there's an anvil waiting to fall on my head, a punishment from the fates for having the audacity to achieve something I thought I deserved. I've largely given my life over to luck and privilege, acknowledging that everything I have was made by others, that taking credit would be selfish, and that the wheel of fortune spins arbitrarily. At first blush it looks like zen. It's easy to miss the doubt beneath.

Impostor syndrome is not inherent. While some of us may be more inclined to worry or caution, and while it may be natural to feel anxious at times about your performance at work, what Williams's misguided cheerleaders understood is that self-doubt is often planted from the outside, through structures we all live with but never consented to. I don't remember the first time I was asked to fill out my race on an application. It was likely before "two or more races" became common, and I had to choose one or the other. Nearly every time it felt like superfluous information, but with some applications—for college, for jobs—I heard a voice telling me that reminding faceless administrators of my Indianness would be smart, that I needed all the "help" I could get. This is of course not how affirmative action works, but at some

The paranoia behind impostor syndrome, of being the fool's version of our best selves, is: How do we know we know? Our fears may seem grounded and reasonable, but they could just be a trick. On the other hand, our confidence could be built on nothing.

point I had absorbed both the idea that I could not do this on my own and that what could vault me over the competition was some part of me that had nothing to do with my abilities.

Much like *fool's gold*, the label of impostor is one that's easy to identify with once it's been thrown at you, or even hinted at. You think you are real, and suddenly you see so clearly how you are not. And there are so many ways to be an impostor. In a unipolar society that props up white, cis, straight, able-bodied, rich men at the top, everyone else is some form of an impostor whether they want to be or not, a fool playing at the real thing, fighting to have their inherent value seen along a different scale than "gold" or "not gold." No one has explicitly called me an impostor for going to college or holding a job while being mixed race; no one accused me of only being there because the institution was hard up for half-white half-Indian people. But that suggestion that drawing attention to (or just being honest about) my race could give me a leg up planted a seed in my mind that any success I found in the next four years would come with this qualifier.

Which is why, for far too long, I checked *white* on any applications, which wasn't a lie but also wasn't the truth. I thought that would stave off worries of inadequacy, ensuring that whatever I earned was through my ability alone (which itself ignored the heightened valuation of whiteness that I didn't realize I was trading on). But the problem with most racism is its plausible deniability. You're never quite sure where it is, and as soon as you think you've located it, you're told you were just the best candidate for the job, even as other candidates whose race can't be denied are told they're "the wrong fit." And you zip away the voice telling you it should matter and the voice telling you it shouldn't matter the way they're making it matter. And you wait for the day unconscious bias comes for you.

▾▴▾▴▾

According to David Rickard, professor emeritus of ore geology and geochemistry at Cardiff University, America is built on the lie of fool's gold. The Jamestown settlement in modern-day Virginia was one of many outposts where English and French colonizers looked for gold, spurred by the success of Spanish miners in South America. "The captain of the first expeditionary fleet, Christopher Newport, was so sure that gold was to be found that he insisted that pyrite found near the settlement was real gold and shipped a load back to England," wrote Rickard in a piece for Oxford University Press's blog in 2015. Similarly convinced this was the real deal, English people were inspired by the shipment to settle in Jamestown, and more funding from the government. "The operation has all the characteristics we associate with the idea of fool's gold: a worthless asset believed by some people to be of real value," wrote Rickard. It may have been built on falsehoods, but Jamestown still became Jamestown.

Is it ironic or apt that pyrite's metaphysical properties are supposed to counter all the things that cause impostor syndrome? The stone's name is derived from the Greek word for "fire," due to how it sparks when struck with other rocks, and all the properties attributed to it involve fire as a metaphor for passion and drive. Pyrite is used to ritually draw money, power, and luck. It's supposed to help you get over intellectual fatigue by increasing clarity and focus. It's a shot of espresso to your nervous system, bolstering you to accomplish what you may have been too afraid to do. It is, essentially, the "male" reaction to impostor syndrome. Commonly it's used in spells for one's career, surrounded by green candles, or in times when a confidence boost is all that stands between you and what you want.

A common cure for feeling like an impostor is "fake it 'til you make it," and pyrite can do just that. The stone does this cool thing called pseudomorphing, aka mineral replacement, in which it takes over another structure, expanding into and replacing the original material until you get something that looks like a seashell but is entirely made of shimmering pyrite—a better and stronger specimen than the original. Another metaphysical property of pyrite is that it can help one overcome bad habits by creating new and healthier patterns. Those patterns already exist. All you need to do is slip yourself into their mold.

In my ninth-grade English class we studied the Bible because, we were told, an understanding of the stories of Christianity would allow us a better understanding of the Western canon, and because I attended a Quaker school and that had to be part of the deal. At some point we discussed Pascal's wager, or the theory that any rational person should believe in (Christian) God, because if there was a god you'd receive infinite rewards in Heaven, and if there wasn't, well, you wouldn't lose much on earth. Which obviously depends on what sort of Christian god you're fake-believing in, because if I spent my life abstaining from sex and drink and impure thoughts and found out on my deathbed that eternal joy and salvation wasn't coming, I'd be pissed.

Pascal's wager raised the question of what to do if you simply couldn't make yourself believe in God. Blaise Pascal argued that acting like you believed would eventually make it so and, thus, to look to other believers and mimic them. "Follow the way by which they began; by acting as if they believed, taking the holy water, having masses said, etc. Even this will naturally make you believe, and deaden your acuteness," he wrote (in French). Pascal was French and Catholic, so perhaps he was primed to see going through the motions of ritual and tradition as belief in and of itself, or at least part of it, rather than the very Protestant idea that one must have a personal, unshakable relationship with God. But as a teenage atheist, the whole idea infuriated me. God, belief, and religion were all absolutes, and aside from not thinking God was real, I also figured if God were real, their omnipotence would not be tricked by your taking communion and saying Hail Marys without really meaning it. If God did exist, they'd probably see through your bullshit.

Pascal's wager could presumably work the other way. If someone were so resolute in their belief in a Christian god but did not go to church or study the Bible or pray, did not play the part, would they lose their faith? That, I guess, is the unanswered question behind all of religion. The wager assumes a divide between actions and beliefs, but also understands they can be united, one way or another. Maybe the women of Clance's study were perceived as competent because they were always sharp and hard-working, or maybe they pretended to know things until they learned them. It is impossible to ever know which is which. Functionally, they're one and the same.

Being a fake isn't so bad. The underlying assumption of the name *fool's gold* is that pyrite isn't gold but that it should be, even though it's just fine as itself. The paranoia comes not from what you are, but from what others think you should be, and from the attempt to separate being enough for yourself from being enough for someone else. Pyrite is supposed to give you that extra fire you need to get over your own paranoia, to just be whoever it is you're trying to be, even if at times it feels unnatural. Because that's pyrite's nature. By being something else—gold, seashells, ore that will transform into something more useful—pyrite is being itself.

▼▲▼▲

In tarot, the Fool is the card of new beginnings. Traditionally we see him depicted with a bindle on his back and a dog by his side, face to the sunny sky, completely unaware that he is about to step off a cliff and plummet to his death or great dismemberment. At first glance it's a card of warning, but the foolishness comes from thinking we know what will happen next. We don't know that his next footstep will catapult him forward. For all we know, he stops and takes in the view before turning around and doing something else. The Fool is also card zero in the storyline of the major arcana, the beginning of the beginning, nothing but potential. He represents the start of a journey and the bravery one needs to begin. After all, declaring a desire for something new always feels a bit silly. He is willing to look like he doesn't know anything—like a fraud, like a fool—in order to get where he wants to go.

High-school English class was also a time for the great fakes and fools of literature. I think of Gatsby's grand, uncut library and how to his guests it was at once proof of his fraud and his authenticity. I assume that's partially why he kept it around, to have a reminder of everything he wasn't and would never be despite everything he was. I think of the foils in Shakespeare who fall backward into luck and romance, mostly because they're mistaken for someone else. And I think of Holly Golightly being a "real phony," at once an intentional construction of a personality and entirely who she was, the weak shell almost entirely eaten away by the brassy shine of herself.

My English teachers were probably so concerned with authenticity and self-awareness in narrative because my peers and I were busy building ourselves, and we weren't going to absorb such obvious advice as "don't be a lying sack of shit" from our elders. But the literary lesson they always imparted was that the real is more important than the fake, that the scam was what did Gatsby and Holly and possibly Pascal in. But Gatsby was Gatsby and Holly was Holly not in spite of their morphing and shifting, but because of it. And though things might not have turned out great for them, I'm not sure the lives they were running away from would have served them any better. Either way, their fates were not a matter of authenticity, or a lack thereof.

Maybe our teachers were preparing us to understand that what we valued in ourselves would not always be what others value. A cave can be filled with gorgeous veins of pyrite, and some people will only see a lack of gold, which has value only because, generations ago, colonizers declared it the valuable thing. The real tension in our lives would come from learning how to work through that.

Impostor syndrome doesn't leave much room for pseudomorphing. It asks us to cast ourselves as one or the other, immediately a success or immediately a failure, without the ability to change and evolve into the thing we're striving to be. Code-switching, gender performance, saying things around friends that you wouldn't say around family—in the world of impostor syndrome these are all proof of being a fake. It presupposes there's one authentic thing to be, and you're not it. But there has to be a consequence to defining yourself in the negative for so long, of thinking of yourself foremost by what you aren't, rather than what you are.

This might sound obvious because we're talking about an inanimate mineral, but pyrite doesn't know how valuable it is or isn't. It's just there, in the rock, in the cave, glinting and growing. I wonder what it would feel like to not only be unaware of what others think, but to not even know the criteria. To act with only my intuition about what is right and wrong, what I can do and what I need help with, and what I will have to sacrifice for the sake of those around me. It would be impossible, and I'm not even sure desirable, to see worth and value as objectives that can be unearthed beneath the biases and expectations of others. Things have value because we say they do. We create the fools.

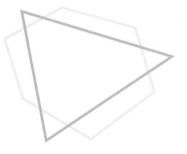

CARNELIAN
and the
Curse of
Positive
Thinking

Carnelian

DESCRIPTION:

The reddish variety of chalcedony,
a mineral made of silica, that gets its
color from iron dioxide in its structure

COMPOSITION:

Silicon dioxide (SiO_2)

METAPHYSICAL PROPERTIES:

The stone of communication and
public speaking, imbuing the user with
eloquence and confidence. It also dispels
negative thoughts and depression.

Carnelian has many faces. When it's brittle and a darker shade of red, it's known as sard. When it's any other color besides reddish-orange, it's chalcedony. When it's layered with black and white, it's sardonyx. Sometimes agates are dyed, heat-treated, and sold as carnelian. Sometimes carnelian is classified as jasper.

These are mostly visual and not geological distinctions—all these stones are part of the cryptocrystalline quartz family and colored by iron dioxide. But real carnelian is rare, at once soft and vivid, with a slight translucence that makes it glow. Like a storm on Jupiter. Like a pooled bead of blood.

These are stones of optimism and energy. They hold the promise that, with their help, you can make your best self known. Carnelian in particular is a stone of communication that promotes eloquence and clarity and helps timid speakers become bold. It was traditionally used by the Assyrians and the Romans in signet rings and seals, a final blessing on a waxed letter to ensure the message got across. The Prophet Mohammed was said to have worn carnelian set in silver on his right hand to bring him luck and to turn away envy. A few sources say Vikings wore it to ease the stress of sacking villages. (You know how hard that can be). It's sometimes called the Singer's Stone, a tool to make one's voice more precise and beautiful.

There are two ways crystals tend to accomplish their goals: welcoming in the positive or fighting off the negative. Carnelian is a bit of both, doing the latter to invite the former. To make you a powerful public speaker or accomplished singer, it clears away the dirty, raw emotions that inhibit elocution. Carnelian gives you the power to still your anger and jealousy, to dispel apathy, envy, and resentment, and to overcome negative feelings and thoughts so your better feelings can shine and you can live a more positive life.

But the language around carnelian insists that, whatever your problems, surmounting them is a matter of personal action. *You* are the problem, and if you're feeling petty or envious, if life seems too hard, if—as some have astoundingly suggested—you're having a hard time getting over abuse, it's because you have the wrong attitude. Saint Hildegard said as much in *Physica*: "If you're so sick you're mad from it, just put a sard on top of your hat and say 'Just as god threw the first angel into the abyss, so may he cut this illness from you and restore good knowledge.'" It doesn't matter what's causing the illness. Have you tried getting rid of it and just not feeling this way? Pull up those bootstraps, baby, you're only bringing yourself down.

▼▲▼▲▼

Few of us have as much to complain about as Epictetus did. Epictectus means "gained" or "acquired" in Greek, a little on the nose for a child born to slavery in Phrygia (modern-day Turkey) in the first century AD. Epictectus was eventually traded to a wealthy man in Rome who worked as a secretary to Nero, who was as benevolent as anyone who owns another person can be, and who allowed Epictetus to study Stoic philosophy. Eventually, Epictetus began lecturing. It sounds like things turned out mostly fine for him, but his name labeled him as a thing to be owned, someone who inherently belonged to anyone but himself. It's safe to assume that this informed his enduring works, which deal with self-management and personal freedom; when you are owned, the only tool you have is your perspective.

Epictetus was full of declarations about the power of the human mind. "It is not events that disturb people, it is their judgments concerning them," he says in his *Enchiridion*. That's as true for spilled wine as it is for your child's death. "Whenever you see someone in tears, distraught because they are parted from a child, or have met with some material loss, be careful lest the impression move you to believe that their circumstances are truly bad." Empathize with them, sure, but remember you have no control, it is all God's will, therefore there is no logic to despair. He makes similar proclamations in his *Discourses*. "I must die, but must I die bawling?" he asks. "I must be put in chains—but moaning and groaning too? I must be exiled; but is there anything to keep me from going with a smile, calm, and self-possessed?"

Americans, with our idea of manifest destiny and our Puritanical work ethic, are particularly primed to accept that "I" am the only person who can solve a problem. The New Thought movement, also known as the "mind cure movement," was founded in America in the nineteenth century largely on the principle that all sickness originates in the mind, and that the right thinking will heal you. It combined Christian ideas, Emersonian individualism, idealism, and spiritualism—basically any tradition that buttressed their thesis that what goes on in the mind has real-world ramifications. "The leaders in this faith have had an intuitive belief in the all-saving power of healthy-minded attitudes as such, in the conquering efficacy of courage, hope, and trust, and a correlative contempt for doubt, fear, worry, and all nervously precautionary states of mind," wrote William James in 1902 in *The Varieties of Religious Experience.*

The movement was founded and influenced by Phineas Quimby, an inventor, mesmerist, and "magnetizer" (a term for those who manipulate magnetic fluids to create a magnetic effect on other people) who believed in the unseen force tying together all living things. The mind, he thought, was just getting in the way, and ultimately, the truth will set us all free. (His teachings supposedly influenced Mary Baker Eddy, the founder of Christian Science.) "The trouble is in the mind, for the body is only the house for the mind to dwell in, and we put a value on it according to its worth. Therefore if your mind has been deceived by some invisible enemy into a belief, you have put it into the form of a disease, with or without your knowledge," he wrote of his treatments. "This I do partly mentally, and partly by talking till I correct the wrong impression and establish the Truth, and the Truth is the cure."

What he's basically talking about is the Serenity Prayer—figuring out what your problems are, accepting with grace the things you cannot change, and gaining the power to change the things you can, even if the only thing you can change is your outlook. Quimby acknowledged that thoughts certainly affect how people behave, but also that they are chemical. The brain is just an organ after all, affected by hormones and vitamins and stimuli as much as the lungs are. Maybe those fickle negative thoughts exist the way a muscle cramp exists, but heavens, don't give them any power. There are *real* problems to be dealt with.

Epictetus speaks of people who can't shore themselves up against the hardships of life, who don't keep their "proper character" as they face hardship or depression, as wolves, lions, and foxes—animalistic beings that have lost all their dignity. "See that you don't turn out like one of those unfortunates," he warns. When asked how he himself accepts the chains and the exile without making an emotional fool of himself, he simply says, "I refuse." He has no advice for how to avoid turning into a malicious, wild fox, just the deep knowledge that you should avoid doing so at all costs or you'll suffer dire philosophical consequences. What's more, those consequences appear to be the same no matter the battle, whether you're upset about being a slave or because your serotonin receptors aren't firing properly. One seems like something Epictetus could've started a revolution over. The other, though, seems to invite the Stoic equivalent of "walk it off." Just put the carnelian on your head and tell yourself your problems aren't really problems.

Epictetus influenced everyone from the U.S. military to author Tom Wolfe, and his works were the foundation of rational emotive behavior therapy, an early form of cognitive behavioral therapy that attempted to help patients identify their "irrational" behaviors and move through their feelings toward a more rational state. But without deeper analysis, the call for positive thinking, of lifting oneself out of despair by one's bootstraps, only works in tautologies. In his manuscripts, Quimby writes of the "two sciences"—one of reality and one of spirituality—and a hypothetical child with head pain: "The child has no idea what it is, and if the mother is as ignorant of its origin as the child, no effect of any moment is produced." Things only get worse if a diagnosis is made, which stresses the child out, but if no one does anything the child supposedly gets better on their own. Quimby's services, then, are to prove that it was all in the kid's head. "If the mother employs me I prove my theory and the child gets well. If [the doctors] prove theirs they kill the child, and an examination is made which establishes their theory, and I am a humbug or quack. If I take the case, and the child gets well, the child was not sick, only a little nervous." This is a real philosophical stretch. Quimby's medicine works only if the child is indeed nervous, not gravely ill. At the very least, with Quimby's services, the child might feel better about himself until the undiagnosed dropsy makes him drop dead.

Some of Quimby's and Epictetus's "cures" were more sound than others—it's a decent idea to try to keep an optimistic attitude in difficult circumstances and to seriously address thoughts of self-harm, less so to assume you can think away a tumor. However, both men acknowledged that patients needed to accept their reality first. Your outlook doesn't get rid of slavery; it only saves you some misery. Soon after the New Thought movement, though, the idea of maintaining a good attitude was weaponized against itself, leading to the persistent belief that you can see your way out of depression, trauma, and institutionalized oppression through the power of positive thinking. As Hettie O'Brien writes in a 2019 report on mindfulness for the *New Statesman*, it is the "perfect coping mechanism for neoliberal capitalism: it privatizes stress and encourages people to locate the root of mental ailments in their own work ethic. As a psychological strategy it promotes a particular form of revolution, one that takes place within the heads of individuals fixated on self-transformation, rather than as a struggle to overcome collective suffering." One just has to *be confident!* and *radiate positive vibes!* to not only face one's problems but to obliterate them. No longer is the "cure" merely influenced by one's attitude; now the assumption is that attitude alone is what's keeping someone down.

The worst thing you can do in any of these instances is feel bad. Bad things can be happening to you, but to feel them is to admit defeat. The only solution is to get rid of any part of you that could get in the way of happiness.

▼▲▼▲▼

Carnelian is a particularly good stone for stamps. It's easily carvable, falling somewhere around seven on the Mohs hardness scale (talc is one; diamond is ten), and hot wax doesn't stick to it. Museums are filled with rings and stamps carved with the images of reversed cattle, hollow faces, and backward letters that only make sense if you imagine their imprint. Carving carnelian is not about building an understandable

Carnelian gives you the power to still your anger and jealousy, to dispel apathy, envy, and resentment, and to overcome negative feelings and thoughts so your better feelings can shine and you can live a more positive life.

image, but about hollowing the stone so it only exists to give shape to something else. Carnelian was also supposedly one of the stones (in some translations the first, in others the sixth) in the breastplate of Aaron, the Jewish high priest of Jerusalem, and represents the blood of the martyrs. To get your message across, all you have to do is sacrifice yourself or carve yourself up, become the inverse so you can make an impression.

Positive thinking seems to demand self-sacrifice, or at least delusion. In *The Book of Mormon*, a musical about the absurdity of faith, a group of elders sings about the horrible things that have happened in their lives and how Mormonism teaches them to, according to the song's title, "Turn It Off." "When you start to get confused because of thoughts in your head," sings Elder McKinley, "don't feel those feelings! Hold them in instead." The song cheerfully presents scenarios to grin and bear it through—a sister dying of cancer, an abusive father, repressed desire for another man. The joke of the song is that this doesn't work, and by the end of the musical everyone has learned to acknowledge and accept their feelings and have a more mature, complex relationship with their faith.

When it comes to positive thinking, few inspirational guides talk about the most crucial point: how to not feel a negative feeling. Some crystal resources say carnelian can help redirect energy, taking your focus away from the negative, whether that's an enemy or a part of your own psyche, and aiming it at something more self-serving instead. Like attracts like, after all, so being happy and confident will only draw more of that toward you. Negativity is spoken of as a poison to be sucked out, and the carnelian can remind you that technically, you do have a choice to not spend all your time dwelling on the negative. But while varying behavioral therapies encourage looking negativity in the face, carnelian's powers only show you how to wield a carving knife and cut away the tougher parts of yourself that aren't serving you.

I have inherited my armor from those who came before me. My mother's mother, my Amma, called outright displays of negative emotion "ugly." She always seemed to be in living in the tense space between who she once was—a poor, tough farm girl from Virginia—and what she later became—a college-educated woman who socialized with the well-heeled, professionally coiffed, and bejeweled women of Princeton, New Jersey. She contained glorious multitudes, but her upbringing gave her little patience for anyone who got caught up in their emotions. My other grandmother, my Didu, moved from India to Germany to get a PhD when she was twenty-four, leaving two young sons with her parents to experience deep cold for the first time and to study in a language she had to learn simultaneously. She later moved with her boys to America, which hadn't been introduced to the sitar by the Beatles yet. On her first day as a zoology professor at a private college, she was assumed to be the cleaning woman. My Didu was always underestimated because of her gender and her race, but when she talks about it, she also shrugs it off. It was what it was. There's so much unspoken trauma in these stories. I feel it in my bones and have picked up on the whispers and silent nods over the years, even though no one has given me a straight story yet. A straight story would perhaps let me see this inherited pain more clearly, to understand it without the carnelian trick cutting it away entirely. But the options seem to be: carry on, or be dragged down by the weight of generations.

I've had fights with every loved one about asking for help. In middle school I refused to ask my friends if we could watch anything but scary movies because all they did was make me cry. In high school I refused to let my mom look at my French homework (a language she was fluent in) or edit my essays (her literal job). I also wouldn't tell her when my World History grades had slipped into the D range. In relationships—romantic and not—I'm unable to bring up problems as they're happening, choosing instead to pretend they're no big deal until I inevitably break down. In each instance I've been asked, why I didn't ask for help if I was struggling? Why didn't I just say something before it got so bad? I don't have an answer, only that for as long as I can remember, asking for help has felt akin to cheating. I'd be admitting defeat if I acknowledged that I forgot the gender of certain French nouns, much less anything else about my life—that I didn't know how to properly communicate a problem, that I was sad sometimes when there was nothing obvious causing it, that at some point I lost the ability to even identify when I had a problem because the only direction in my head was through. Go through.

My problem is my inability to act, more than anyone else's inability to act toward me. It is embarrassing to fail, but other people never got help, so why should I? The dark promise of carnelian has always made sense to me. Whatever mess I'm in, it's mine to get out of. I just need to try harder, do better, be happier, "Turn It Off," and I'll be known. I was convinced that my force of will was all I needed, and if something was bad I just had to find a solution, alone. Most of the time, that still feels like the truth.

In high school, at the peak of my refusal to ask for help, my school hosted a "Diversity Day," when classes were replaced with workshops about our identities, the hardships different kinds of people face, and what we could do separately and together to help each other. I didn't go to any of the groups for people of color and only reluctantly chose one about reproductive rights. I remember looking at the black and brown people on the bus on my way home from school that day and thinking of racism, and then being furious that the thought occurred to me. If my school hadn't brought it up, I reasoned, it wouldn't be an issue. I had not yet faced violent racism myself and had not learned to identify the benevolent kind that I now know had surrounded me then. I really thought if I ignored it, it wouldn't exist.

It took me until I was in my mid-twenties to identify as a feminist and a person of color. It's not that I didn't think of myself as a woman or as the child of an Indian immigrant. One of my first memories is noticing the contrast of my paler skin against my dad's darker skin as he held me in the shower, knowing already that some people would be mad at him for having skin like his, but not understanding why. But to acknowledge there are things the world sees as a problem that I can't fix was not an option. My ancestors cut out deep parts of themselves. They crossed oceans, forgot languages, dressed to match the world around them, and adopted new prejudices in order to spare me the impact of their otherness. I was, and sometimes am, reluctant to identify with the more marginalized parts of myself, even though they fought so hard to survive. Sometimes, "stay positive" sounds like other things—stay white, stay straight, stay rich, stay sane. Don't admit there are other parts to you, the parts that we left behind on the carving room floor.

For many people, acknowledging that there are societal structures in place to keep certain people oppressed can be freeing. Not that they're not worth fighting against, but this acknowledgment is an important explanation for why things are so hard for so many. But for a long time, I only thought of that explanation as an excuse, a cheat code that led everyone who wasn't a straight white man to develop a horrible victim complex. Acknowledging there may be other forces at play to make my life difficult felt akin to asking for help on my homework—admitting there's any problem means admitting you haven't been able to solve it, that your bootstraps couldn't take the effort of your hoisting, and that you don't have as much power as you want. And it's in the best interest of the keepers of those societal structures to make recognizing institutional oppression feel like an excuse, to make it feel like you're whining about not getting what you want instead of recognizing that you've been kept from things you deserve. Everything feels like cheating.

My partner also comes from people who faced hardship and found a way to thrive, but from people who are much more ready to admit when there's a problem, even when that problem is in their head. When bad things happen to my partner, when they get depressed, they groan, they stomp, they complain. When we were first together, I didn't know how to handle their holistic despair. At my worst I intentionally ignored what they were talking about, silently breathing or distracting myself with some task, because to acknowledge a problem would be to make it real, and give it power I don't want it to have. But even at my best I was dismissive, suggesting solutions instead of letting my partner cry, offering to go on a walk, to go to a movie, anything to change the topic from grief that has no cause, that only leaves when it is ready.

My personal brand of positive thinking is there's no use in crying, so just figure out what you can do. I have never been a good wallower. I need hope to propel me forward. I need something to do, something to fix, or just something to offer in the face of sadness and decay. My version of depression is often cured by taking a long walk or doing something to get out of my head. Sometimes the bootstraps work for me, but I have to remember that I shouldn't always have to use them.

▼▲▼▲

In 1834, *Working Man's Advocate* published a joke about the man who claimed to have invented the perpetual motion machine. "It is conjectured that Mr. Murphee will now be enabled to hand himself over the Cumberland river or a barn yard fence by the straps of his boots," they wrote, the idea as absurd as a machine that never stops moving. For much of the nineteenth century, the phrase "pull yourself up by your bootstraps" was used to illustrate the ridiculousness of thinking one could do the impossible. It wasn't until the 1920s (many point to James Joyce's *Ulysses* as the turning point) that the idea of hoisting oneself off the ground by one's bootstraps was not only possible, but necessary. That you alone could fix your problems if you were strong enough. Because the other option is that we are powerless, with only our thoughts to give us the illusion of action.

The tricky part of the Serenity Prayer is when you ask for the wisdom to know the difference between what you can and can't change. There is no objective difference; one person's battle is another person's accepted reality. At its worst, carnelian guilts you into thinking it's all in your head—just leave him, just stop being sad, just do the impossible. But at its best, carnelian can bring us that wisdom. There are days when you can't give in, and carnelian is alluring because it reminds us that fighting back is possible. No matter the situation, there is always something else we could technically be doing to change it. Carnelian supposedly gives you not just the confidence to act in your best interest, to rip the Band-Aid off and do what's best, but also the power to ignore the parts of you that are afraid of the consequences. Apply carnelian to everything and the crystal loses its power, but use it in moderation and sometimes it's right.

Part of carnelian's powers is fighting against envy. Keep your thoughts on yourself and your situation instead of dwelling on what other people have that you don't. Positive thinking means worrying only about yourself, while negative thinking means being distracted by the world. But positive thinking can only work when you understand the whole; the world is not a distraction, and allowing yourself to see the negative, the envy, and the abuse means you are seeing the world clearly, for what it is. There is freedom in integrating the positive with the negative, in acknowledging what you are and what you aren't, in remaining whole instead of cutting away the undesirable parts of yourself.

I would rather keep myself whole. When I hold my carnelian, I want to invoke all the ways I can keep myself afloat while acknowledging what lurks beneath the surface. I want it to give me the power to turn my positive thoughts into actions, to not mistake my attitude for praxis. But most of all, I want to stay positive while acknowledging the fullness of myself, every problem, every mindset. Nothing deserves to be erased. My carnelian is not set in a ring or etched with new images. It is whole, an image only of itself, and I am reminded that positive thinking doesn't require that I be hollowed out. I don't need to be carved to be beautiful.

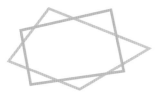

CITRINE
and the
Cost of
Happiness

Citrine

DESCRIPTION:

A yellow-brown type of quartz
sometimes confused with topaz

COMPOSITION:

Silicon dioxide (SiO_2)

METAPHYSICAL PROPERTIES:

Thought to bring happiness and success,
especially in money matters. Also used
to boost self-esteem and confidence.

n the '90s, the worst thing you could do was sell out. As a child, I didn't have anything to sell, much less anyone to sell it to, but I spat the insult like venom whenever someone did something my peers deemed "too mainstream," even within our eighth-grade halls. You were a sellout if you went to the wrong park, if you shopped at the wrong places, if you got lunch from the wrong deli. I can't even remember all the rules now.

Though I used the phrase against others too, I was called a sellout for listening to pop punk. Or, rather, the bands I liked were sellouts, and I was a sellout by proxy. Pop punk fit the sellout label perfectly—the genre was just as ambiguous as the insult. It obviously lacked the integrity of anarchy and anti-capitalism, but still sneered at politicians and corporations in a way the pop music of the time wouldn't. The bands I listened to also complained about sellouts, sometimes dismissing whole genres outright, despite their bank-sponsored tours. This was all too much for a sheltered and privileged teenager to understand, so without a dictionary definition, I gathered that the biggest complaint against sellouts was that these people made money.

No one stopped to specify the difference between making money while maintaining your integrity and completely changing your sound and vision solely for the promise of cash. There was little nuance around the idea that in a capitalist society, you still need money to survive, and only the most privileged or daring could live off the kindness of others. Money, fame, all the traditional trappings of success were viewed with suspicion.

But in 1997, Everclear briefly—and probably unintentionally—complicated the idea of the sellout in their song "I Will Buy You a New Life." The song is a promise to an ex that things will get better, that he'll give her the house and the car and the garden she always wanted as soon as he can pay for it. In it, the singer, Art Alexakis, sneers at anyone who'd look down on doing anything for the money, saying they only condescend because they've never had to go without, they've never woken up to a "welfare Christmas." His verses imply that only the most privileged can worry about a label like sellout.

Alexakis probably had reason to be annoyed with his pop-punk contemporaries. After his father left him and his four siblings, his mother relocated them to housing projects from the more comfortable suburbs of LA. His brother died of a heroin overdose. Alexakis was abused and raped and tried to kill himself. Money wouldn't have guaranteed that none of thiswould have happened, but it might have helped. This is one of those instances in which everyone was right. Alexakis was right to call out those who would criticize materialism from their comfortable perches, who didn't understand everything contained within the promise of being able to provide a "perfect, shiny, and new" house to someone they loved. But money was still the root of all that killed; its existence, and the lack of it, was what led to the "welfare Christmas." And the conflation of happiness and success with wealth still keeps us all trapped.

◥◣◥◣◥◣

Citrine, clear with shades of yellow and brown like a crackling sun, is known as both the "success stone" and the "merchant's stone" and is used for its properties relating to wealth and prosperity. Most crystals known for their money work are green, for the obvious associations, but citrine feels more like warm gold, the difference between rolling on a bed of dollar bills and diving like Scrooge McDuck into a sea of coins that magically give way to your flesh. Crystal guides encourage business owners to place a citrine in their cash registers to keep money flowing. Money is its own form of energy, and citrine helps you harness it for your benefit, to shift from a mindset of scarcity to one of plenty. At the same time the stone is supposed to emanate joy and positivity. It gives you the power to transform your wildest wishes into reality and radiates such positive energy that it never needs to be grounded or cleansed. If your wishes are related to your finances (and whose aren't, most of the time?) it will help you not just attract wealth but maintain it. Its properties imply that happiness, money, success, and abundance are all the same. If you want one, surely it will come with the rest. In fact, it must.

As to why this is the case, the history is murky. Some believe citrine to be one of the stones in Aaron's breastplate in Exodus, but that story doesn't assign any metaphysical meaning to the citrine, and there are scant other myths about it. The trick of putting it in your cash box has been attributed to everyone from the Chinese to the Brazilians. Even in Hellenistic Greece it was used largely as a decorative stone. But in modern times, crystal healers have all seemingly agreed that citrine brings joy, positivity, and financial abundance.

In our modern capitalist hellscape, it's hard to know what success looks like without money. Success means graduating from college, which costs money to attend. In my work, I gather that I'm successful the more someone wants to pay me for my words. Success is winning a contest. Success is being able to buy gifts for those you love. Success is a promotion. Falling in love, cherishing a friend, feeling emotionally fulfilled—those are the successes that aren't quite recognized, aren't quite believed. Sure, they're great, but wouldn't they be even better with money behind them? With a stable job? You wouldn't have to worry. In other words: you're happy, but you'd be happier with all that and money, too.

Money magic in modern Wicca and other practices sounds plainly absurd most of the time. Spells designed to draw wealth refer to the "abundance mindset," an idea that if you act like you have money to burn, the universe will make it so. Radically, these spells remind us that money is not a finite resource, and in fact is societally constructed. But instead of suggesting getting rid of the system altogether, they offer tips on how to game it. In these spells, being generous with your money will inspire the world to be generous back to you. So you tip $20 to your bodega guy, give all your change to the homeless, and light a green candle next to your citrine in honor of your actions, to prove that you're a giving person. Financial security can be yours as long as you show the spirits you're worthy.

While it may be ridiculous to think that you're poor because you haven't been giving enough money away, it's slightly better than an even more loaded thesis in American money magic: you're poor because you've sinned. Beginning in the 1880s, Baptist minister (among other things) Russell Conwell began touring America and preaching his sermon "Acres of Diamonds." It began with a story of a man so obsessed with finding wealth that he searched the world for money and died frustrated and poor, only for others to find out the meager piece of land he lived on was full of diamonds the whole time. You'd think this would set up a sermon about appreciating what you have and how the pursuit of wealth is destructive, but you'd be wrong. To Conwell, this man was "discontented because he feared he was poor," and thus the solution was a kind of spell—believe you will become rich, and it will happen.

The stakes couldn't have been higher for Conwell. Getting wealthy wasn't just possible, it was a duty from God. He railed against straw men who said the rich were greedy and dishonest. "My friend, that is the reason why you have [no money], because you have that idea of people . . . ninety-eight out of one hundred of the rich men of America are honest. That is why they are rich." He preached that money is power, and good could only be done with money. "Money printed your Bible, money builds your churches, money sends your missionaries, and money pays your preachers," he argued. Most importantly, he reminded his audience that if richness was next to godliness, then poverty was a sin. When imagining someone asking him the question of whether we should be sympathetic to the poor, he said, "To sympathize with a man whom God has punished for his sins, thus to help him when God would still continue a just punishment, is to do wrong, no doubt about it, and we do that more than we help those who are deserving. While we should sympathize with God's poor—that is, those who cannot help themselves—let us remember that there is not a poor person in the United States who was not made poor by his own shortcomings, or by the shortcomings of someone else. It is all wrong to be poor, anyhow."

Conwell grew up poor. In *The Life of Russell H. Conwell*, a fawning and probably horribly biased biography of Conwell, author Albert H. Smith notes that Conwell's parents, Martin Conwell and Miranda Wickham, "started life together on a capital [Martin] had earned of $200," doing stonemason work and farming in the Berkshires. He attributes the minister's Emersonian self-reliance to his hardscrabble life in the mountains. He paints a picture of a rambunctious, empathetic, misunderstood boy who grew up in a three-room house with no stove. Miranda supplemented the family income by making suspenders and coats, and "no applicant for charity ever went hungry from her door if

In our modern
capitalist
hellscape, it's
hard to know
what success
looks like
without money.

there was the least evidence of worthiness in his manner." An apocryphal story says their home was part of the Underground Railroad and that one night Conwell awoke to see his father and Frederick Douglass conversing outside. Conwell attended Wilbraham Wesleyan Academy, and then Yale, and though his parents were too poor to pay for much and he had to work to pay his way through school, he seemed to have the disposition of someone who feels guilty about their place in the world, the child of a self-made man (or the closest you can get to one; no such thing exists) who worries he is living on stolen valor and wants to prove himself worthy.

Andrew Carnegie also grew up poor, the son of Scottish weavers who moved to Pennsylvania to escape extreme poverty. Young Carnegie was sent to work in a cotton mill six days a week. He grew up, invested in oil, made an astronomical fortune, and then wrote a foundational text for anyone who thinks greed is good. In "The Gospel of Wealth," he writes that the world has never seen such an incredible standard of living as it had in those modern times. Who cares if it is only available to a few? "It is well, nay, essential, for the progress of the race that the houses of some should be homes for all that is highest and best in literature and the arts, and for all the refinements of civilization, rather than that none should be so," he argues. "Much better this great irregularity than universal squalor."

This disparity, to Carnegie, is progress. Society "must either go forward or fall behind; to stand still is impossible." Carnegie takes it as self-evident truth that men with the talent for running business must do so and must make a profit, and though he implores rich men to donate to charities and open libraries during their lifetimes, he writes that the condition of humanity must be better under this capitalism than it is under any other system. In fact, for Carnegie capitalism is itself civilization, and that is what the anarchists and socialists wish to destroy. We have produced the best life so far under this system, he argues, why uproot it when something better is not guaranteed?

Though "The Gospel of Wealth" is Carnegie's most famous essay, the one bankers and preachers alike use to justify wealth as a moral imperative, "Popular Illusions About Trusts," is the essay in which Carnegie lays out his most obvious argument for money as the bearer of happiness. He writes that the overwhelming tendency toward "aggregation of capital" cannot be stopped, so instead of attempting to restrict what wealth can be made, "we should hail every increase as something gained, not for the few rich, but for the millions of poor. . . . It makes for higher civilization, for the enrichment of human life, not for one, but for all classes of men." It is trickle-down economics at its plainest—a wealthy few means factories, means trains, means it's easier for everyone to have things that only royalty used to have. You may never know what a weekend is at your factory job, but at least everyone can afford multiple shirts.

What makes these texts and others that influenced modern prosperity theology—the spiritual belief that your wealth and health are a direct reflection of your positive relationship with God—so appealing is they admit that being poor sucks. They say poverty is a sign that you are unsuccessful and wasting your potential; you are doing society no good by not making more money. But it is also a sign that you yourself are probably not enjoying life as much as you could be. The prosperity gospel is a version of money magic, positive thinking that focuses on finances as the ultimate reward for goodness. There is no valor in suffering when the possibility of riches exists. Why stay poor when you could be rich, yes, but more important, why stay miserable when you could be happy?

▽△▽△▽

The citrine is an affordable stone. Like many gems, it used to be rarer; Queen Victoria favored it, and during the Art Deco period it was a popular choice for ostentatious jewelry. But discoveries of new mines and advancements in technology turned it from a particularly prized stone into something less special. In fact, although natural citrine is still rare, we figured out how to heat-treat amethyst to turn its purples into yellows and browns. Any quartz can be a citrine if the opportunity arises.

It could be that citrine is associated with wealth because of people like Queen Victoria, though if proximity to royalty is all it took for a stone to bring one money, then every gem would be used for it. But yellow is a happy color. Too bright and it can be overwhelming, but the muted yellow of most citrine feels like the warmth of the sun after a long rain. It's a bright, open daffodil. It's the peak of summer at six p.m., when you're still astounded the sun is nowhere near the horizon, and you're energized anew to stay outside and keep walking and ask your friends *what if we did something we've never done before? What do we have to lose?* Because you're happy, just so deliriously happy that you're alive to see a day like this, and it would be a betrayal of the higher powers and ancestors to waste that.

Being rich feels like that, and if citrine brings us happiness, then wealth must be part of the package. Money magic makes sense to me sometimes. On the days I've had an influx of cash, I feel like raining it down on everyone I love. I want to be the magnanimous host circling the party, refilling everyone's drinks. (Is it any wonder citrine is the color of champagne?) I want to tell my friends to treat themselves to whatever they want, don't worry, it's worth it. I want to offer them shelter, assistance, a clean slate, and bask in their appreciation at how generous I am. How *good* I am. The money only enhances my goodness. What a waste to not have it.

⁜

The argument from my college counselor was that college was a "match to be made, not a prize to be won." A gentler way of saying that not everyone was cut out to get an MBA from an Ivy League school. It was also a cousin phrase to the one our loving, liberal parents often told us:

nothing else matters as long as you're happy. Figure out what you want to do, follow your passion; life isn't worth living unless you do what you love. However, that came with some caveats. What made you happy couldn't involve not going to college. Figuring out what you wanted to do had to come from declaring a major, studying hard, and at least having a degree "to fall back on" if your passion didn't work out. You can't do what you love without money to support yourself, my peers and I were told—and in fact, you'll know you're successful when you have enough to quit your job to do just that. This was good, practical advice for the world we lived in. Our parents and teachers wanted us to have options. They wanted us to live happy lives, which to them meant lives free from worry. The happiness would come with security, safety, and the best chance for a fat bank account. We may have all pretentiously wanted to be starving artists, but our parents knew it's hard to make art on an empty stomach.

I tend to romanticize the years after I graduated from college, with an English degree cum laude, into an economy that was about to crash. I worked as a waitress, spilling martinis onto sidewalk tables and cursing rich men on dates who left five-dollar tips. I became one of those people who asks you if you have time for the environment on the sidewalk, chasing down credit card information so I could make less than minimum wage. I sold olive oil soap to women on the Upper East Side and took odd-shaped ends home for myself so I didn't have to spend three dollars on a bar of Irish Spring. I got an unpaid writing internship. I shared a too-small apartment with only one closet because it was a steal. I frequented bars offering free popcorn and pizza with purchase of a drink so I could get drunk with dinner. I carried home chairs and side tables I found on the sidewalk without thinking of bedbugs (until I got them). This was how it was supposed to go. Live the starving artist life for a little bit, take any work you can get, save, and pay your bills.

The counterpoint to the prosperity gospel is that money can't buy happiness, which is generally true. But in those days nothing felt stable, and when nothing is stable, stability starts looking a lot like joy.

Joy became leaving a writing job because of burnout for a full-time job in a field I didn't want to be in but enforced 9-to-5 hours. Joy became having a partner who was miserable at their engineering job, but who made more than I ever would. We'd do what we wanted someday, but for now things were good, we told ourselves. This is what success looks like.

I'm not saying there's no value in hard work and saving, only that we've tied wealth, success, and happiness so tightly together it's impossible to tell which is which.

I developed nerve pain in my jaw. At first I felt it in just one spot if I tapped it too hard, and then it started to tingle all over my face. I know part of it was stress. I clenched my jaw when I scrolled through Twitter and saw all the ways people were allowed to deny services and resources to marginalized people. It cost twenty dollars to see my doctor about the pain, a few hundred for an MRI, and more for a series of acupuncture sessions to make it go away. I could have ignored it and tried to power through, but if I'm unwell, I can't focus on work. And if I can't work, I can't do the things that make me happy. My health and my happiness are directly tied to my bank account.

Suicide rates have risen in America since 1999, and according to the CDC, nearly half of those who died by suicide had no recorded mental health diagnoses. Instead, the CDC suggests other influencing factors: "job, money, legal, or housing stress." Access to these things is what brings us stability and safety and happiness, and what's keeping so many people from them aren't their choices, but things beyond their control: governments, economies, and prejudices. The sickness is seeping in from the outside. Without a job, without health care for your preexisting conditions, without a safe place to live, without the money to pay for all of those things, how on earth can you be expected to be happy?

There exists the concept of relative happiness, that people in poor societies will find ways to be happy just as people in rich ones do; that money isn't the deciding factor when it comes to emotional and spiritual abundance. There is truth in that. I can say my partner is happier after quitting engineering and devoting themself to cartooning, though they will never make as much as they did designing HVAC systems. I can say I'm happier pursuing a career in the unstable world of writing than anything else my skill set may have prepared me for. Even when the bottom drops out and the thought crosses my mind, *Couldn't we have just done it for the money?* I know that wouldn't have been right.

This isn't the whole story, though. The story is that my college counselor was employed by my private high school. The story is that my family and some scholarships were able to pay for private college. The story is that I write every morning from the balcony of the apartment bought for me by inheritance, and though none of this insulates me from the threat of losing a job or a loved one or my health, boy does it help. There is a shame in not earning, but a bigger shame in not having.

I still feel guilty when I am on the receiving end of someone else's money magic. When I am the one whose drink is being poured, who is being told to treat myself, I feel it is not just generosity coming my way sevenfold. I am a leech accepting handouts, a failure for relying on the kindness of others. How dare I receive help from those who could provide it. Some days, I turn to citrine to alleviate the shame, and some days I know this is just an attempt to ignore my privilege. But the power of citrine is in how it promises to soothe the tension of having in a society where so many people don't. Money does not buy happiness, but it certainly does not disinvite it. In this crystalline money magic, money is not a virtue, nor is it a sin. It is just a fact, something you need to exist. Under capitalism, we're all sellouts.

⩗⩘⩗

A full moon in Capricorn is a time when many witches call for stability and wealth; to put money and citrine on your altar and cast spells for more. Capricorn is a practical and prudent sign, and those born under it are ambitious in a patient and rule-following way—not wildly creative but measured and careful, never acting without understanding exactly what will follow. A Capricorn moon is a time to consider the pentacles suit in the tarot deck, the one that represents the body and the home, work and stability. It is literally represented by a gold coin.

Magic makes an obvious connection between the spiritual and the tangible, but it also treats money as a condition as natural as family or sex or the human body. Not a man-made object, but an ever-present cosmic truth. I wonder who was the first witch to ask the universe for money. I want to know what other abundances in her life didn't feel like enough, if she was content in her hut on the side of town with her garden and familiar and knowledge of healing herbs, and suddenly realized the town was changing and she couldn't just barter her powers for essentials anymore. Maybe she put a coin on her altar as soon as she found one, or maybe the spirits told her the more she wanted (even witches want more) was worth pursuing, and that it wouldn't come any other way.

Citrine, for all it can bring, also carries the assumption that money is inherent. But if there were no such thing as money, what would this particular magic look like? What is a spell for success if there are no bills to pay? If citrine is supposed to help bring you abundance, what might it bring if you didn't need wealth? I want to know what it feels like to have resources to share that weren't gained or bolstered by finances. I want a happiness and peace that isn't affected by a financial safety net. I want my citrine to remind me of the abundance of the sun, warm and shining and something money can neither bring more of nor take away. I want to know what that kind of success looks like, but I don't think I ever will.

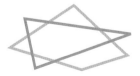

OPALS
and the
Terror of
Change

Opals

DESCRIPTION:

A mineraloid that, in its most
precious forms, displays
dazzling iridescence

COMPOSITION:

A hydrated form of amorphous silica

METAPHYSICAL PROPERTIES:

The "eye stone," allowing the user
total cosmic clarity. Supposedly reflects
the mood of the wearer, and
sometimes amplifies it.

When Kermit first asks, "Why are there so many songs about rainbows?" you can't see him. You hear the plucking of the banjo and see a thicket of dense, dark trees from high above. A lens flare casts a multicolored circle around where we imagine Kermit is sitting, somehow in possession of a banjo even though he is both a frog and in the middle of a swamp, but he is obscured as he declares that rainbows, in their lightness and temporality, have nothing to hide.

The song has little to do with the rest of *The Muppet Movie*, in which Kermit both gathers the rest of the Muppets on his way to California to be a star and is on the run from a man who wants to fry his legs for dinner. It's the closest we come to an "I want" song, something that positions Kermit as introspective and yearning for more—for whatever is at the end of the rainbow, or for the titular rainbow connection that makes us all stop and stare whenever a rainbow appears. But he doesn't know he wants to get out of the swamp until a talent agent tells him he can, and even then, he only wants to do it because it could "make millions of people happy." It's not the fame that motivates him but the friends he finds along the way, a mishmash of weird creatures whose hidden talents he can see and appreciate in a way the rest of the world can't. And he promises "someday" we'll all find this connection. We haven't gotten there yet, we can't see it all right now, but don't worry, we will.

Rainbows are a great metaphor. They mean just about everything, from the roadmap to riches, to the inclusion and celebration of all identities, to God's promise that he will never wipe out life on earth more than once. It could be because of their typical appearance at the end of a storm, with a pot of gold at the end a fitting reward for enduring the turmoil of wetness and thunder, real or metaphorical. We can see them only at certain times, at certain angles, and when they reveal themselves it feels like a cosmic gift. And then there's the color—the full spectrum of visible light on display. A rainbow's power is in revealing every possibility all at once.

Opal has long been valued for its truly fantastic color structure, like a rainbow that has been caught in glass. "Of all precious stones, it is opal that presents the greatest difficulties of description, it displaying at once the piercing fire of carbunculus [garnet], the purple brilliancy of amethystos [amethyst], and the sea-green of smaragdus [emerald], the whole blended together and refulgent with a brightness that is quite incredible," wrote Pliny the Elder. "Some opals carry such resplendent lustre with them that they are able to match the bravest and richest colors of painters: others represent the flaming fire of brimstone, yea and the bright blaze of burning oil." It was the most highly prized stone in the Roman empire at the time Pliny wrote and lends itself to intense mythology worldwide. In Indigenous Australian lore, the opal was created when a butterfly got trapped beneath snow, which leeched the color from her wings and placed it in the mountains. Mayan and Aztec people called the red-orange opals forged from volcanoes in Central America *quetzalitzlipyollitli*, the "bird-of-paradise stone," and lighter opals *vitzitziltecpatl*, the "hummingbird stone," both in honor of quick and colorful creatures that inspire joy and wonder. Like a rainbow, you can never hold them in your hand.

"Rainbow Connection" always makes me cry even though I've watched *The Muppet Movie* dozens of times. I figured it was mostly a trick of the chord progression and any lingering sadness I had about Jim Henson dying too soon. But there's a worry to it. In the last verse, Kermit asks if you, too, have heard voices in your sleep, calling you to the rainbow. "Is this the sweet sound that calls to young sailors?" he asks. If it's a sound the sailors heard, then it's most likely the Sirens singing, birds with the beautiful faces and voices of women whose song inspired seamen to launch themselves overboard. Attempting to find that rainbow connection, one that shines with every color, feels dangerous. Get too close and you'll be driven mad by its overwhelming power. But, Kermit admits, "I've heard it too many times to ignore it. It's something that I'm supposed to be." There is a part of him that is trying to get out and shine, and he is compelled to let it, no matter what dangers might lie ahead.

In the Middle Ages in the west, the opal was thought to possess the special virtues of every gem. It brought the profound luck of having not just every stone's color, but every metaphysical property available to you at the same time, an entire magical arsenal for the price of one. From all our other myths about rainbows, the yearning for them, it seems obvious that a rainbow-colored stone would hold in it the promises of eternity, of vision, and of whatever else makes us write songs about rainbows. But look at it from another angle, and the rainbow looks like a curse. It is too much at once, too many options, each one showing how little any other may matter, how our definitions of ourselves and each other are useless because we are capable of literally anything. We can be many things at once. We can choose many conflicting journeys. The rainbow, the opal, gives us a glimpse of how many ways we can shine, and our narrow idea of our pasts and possible futures are rendered useless. That may not feel like luck.

▼ ▼▲▼

In Sir Walter Scott's 1829 novel *Anne of Geierstein*, an opal reveals a woman to be, perhaps, a witch. Hermione, a mysterious Persian woman, arrives and steals the heart of the Baron of Arnheim. She wears an opal in her hair every day, which darkens when she is upset, brightens when she is happy, and shoots a "little spark, or tongue of flame" when she is in a particular mood. Her handmaids report that she is unusually quiet for a few moments each night after removing it from her hair and that she's always worried about it, as if it were the source of some greater power: "Even in the use of holy water at the door of the church she was observed to omit the sign of the cross on the forehead, for fear, it was supposed, of the water touching the valued jewel."

One day, the baron flicks a few drops of holy water on Hermione's head while entering the church, and "the opal, on which one of these drops had lighted, shot out a brilliant spark like a falling star, and became the instant afterwards lightless and colourless as a common pebble, while the beautiful Baroness sank on the floor of the chapel with a deep sigh of pain." The opal was thought to carry some sort of connection to the devil, which was undone by the blessed water. She was carried to her bed, where the next day nothing but a pile of ash remained.

In *The Curious Lore of Precious Stones*, written in 1913, George Frederick Kunz makes reference to what was, by then, the widely accepted notion that opals are bad luck, something he calls a "foolish modern superstition." Some attributed this to a misreading of *Anne of Geierstein*, and others to other stories, but according to Kunz the beauty of the opal, which was fully appreciated by past generations, was marred only by people looking for something to be afraid of. However, he contradicts himself, as every historic reference he draws on for proof of the power and beauty of the stone implies some sort of trickery. He calls the opal "a fit emblem" of inconstancy in Shakespeare's *Twelfth Night* and quotes Dr. Stephen Batman, writing in the mid-1500s, on how the opal has the power to "Smithe [men] with a maner blindness, that is called Amnetia, so that they may not see neither take heede what is done before their eyen." Still, Kunz calls his nineteenth-century contemporaries "altogether unreasonable—and indeed almost inexplicable" for being wary of the opal. Sure, they may crack all the time. Sure, "black opals" were often cheap, white stones dipped in ink. But how can you resist all the colors and light of the world in one object, which from the moment you hold it begins to decay?

Opals have never quite been able to escape the fear that they bring bad luck. It's in part because they are temperamental and soft. Heat and moisture can change their color and make them crack, and they can scratch when banged against hard surfaces. How disturbing that a rock, a symbol of solidity, is so easily broken. Hermione's main problem was not being a witch, but wearing an opal every day, something most jewelers would now tell you would make the stone crumble right out of its setting. The opal is a beautiful thing, meant to be held at arm's length. Don't look at it, it's too beautiful. Don't touch it, you'll only fuck it up. Don't try to own it, because it will only change on you.

The rainbow is only the spectrum visible to humans. There are butterflies and shrimp and birds that can see ultraviolet light, snakes and frogs that can sense infrared. The lure of the rainbow Kermit sings of is that the rainbow is both everything, and also proof that there is more. We are presented with the limits of our own vision, with how much we fundamentally can't see and that we must figure out how to sense in other ways. For many of us, there is terror in that revelation—however much we want the things, the people, around us to grow and experiment and blossom, we want that to have already happened, and whatever is in front of us to be fixed. You can be whoever you want, but for there to be more than we can see makes us uncomfortable. How uncomfortable, then, is the opal, which is suspected to have the "ability to bring one's traits and characteristics to the surface for examination and transformation," everything that can be seen and everything that was already there but couldn't. It is the "eye stone," which allows you to focus on every aspect of yourself—even what's hidden from you— and helps you to understand clearly that which you'd rather ignore. It is said to amplify every thought and feeling, make the unconscious conscious and ready for examination. It can make you not just multiple things, but everything all at once. It's a knowledge that, sometimes, is too overwhelming to bear.

In *The Bell Jar*, Sylvia Plath wrote of starving at the foot of a metaphorical fig tree because she felt unable to choose which branch she wanted to eat from. "One fig was a husband and a happy home and children, and another fig was a famous poet and another fig was a brilliant professor, and another fig was Ee Gee, the amazing editor, and another fig was Europe and Africa and South America, and another fig was Constantin and Socrates and Attila and a pack of other lovers with queer names and offbeat professions, and another fig was an Olympic lady crew champion, and beyond and above these figs were many more figs I couldn't quite make out," and she wanted them all but couldn't have them. She had to choose one, or maybe a few, but certainly not all. And instead of choosing, she watches as they all wither away.

When I read that passage, what makes me sad is not that she can't have them all, but that she can't choose which she wants, which are related but distinct problems. Because the idea of all is just too overwhelming. I wouldn't know what to do with the husband, professor, and South America figs all in the palm of my hand. Instead, I like the act of choosing. Ideally it's easy, with one fig looking so ripe and sweet that all thoughts of how the others might taste disappear. But even when it isn't, a choice is an act of control. An unknown fig can't fall

The rainbow, the opal, gives us a glimpse of how many ways we can shine, and our narrow idea of our pasts and possible futures are rendered useless. That may not feel like luck.

on your head if you had the wherewithal to pick it first. There are no surprises when you know what you're doing.

At first glance the promise of the opal seems to be the clarity and intuition to understand what you're choosing. When you can see every option before you, there's nothing unknown, and you can step forward with the confidence that you foresaw all the consequences. Of course, when you see everything you also see all the fruit you didn't eat, and even if you're happy with the figs you have, every choice you make cuts another one off. Every choice is a little death, a facet of yourself that won't get to shine. It's a small sacrifice to make, though, for the comfort of building and enforcing a solid reality. It's a way to turn the rainbow illusion into something real.

The opal is also a good stone for people of independent spirit, for those who "wish to live by their own rules," which would seem in opposition to a stone that lets you see the world clearly enough to build a sturdy life. Free spirits typically don't take to staying on one path. But there is nothing more independent than making your own choices, by yourself, free of influence. To be independent means having a life where nothing else can touch you, where you can keep moving if you sense a shadow creeping up behind you, where the fruit doesn't weigh you down. Where you never have to acknowledge that your choices aren't the only things that affect you. Where you never have to reckon with the parts of the spectrum you can't see.

I have a bad habit of running away with a plan on first suggestion and taking the present as a constant. An idea turns into a promise, something I can rely on and shape my life around instead of a temporary flash. More than once, my partner has had to talk me down from hyperventilating over the smallest changes in a plan (or not even changes, because the only plan that existed was one I began making up without telling anyone). Sometimes I lie in bed and ask my partner what they would do in unlikely situations. What if tomorrow you wanted kids and I didn't? What if we have to move in with our parents? What would you do if we could never have sex again? What if you change your mind? And I'm never satisfied when the answer is, "I don't know, but we'll figure it out together," which is always what it is. I demand to know every outcome for every possibility so I know the edges of what my life can be. Because infinity is terrifying. If you can do anything, then who are you? How can you define your life, yourself, when you have no boundaries?

A joke I make whenever I'm watching a movie or show that involves a surprise party is that I'd hate to have a surprise party. It seems in line with my character as someone who likes to know what's going on, someone who gets anxious over guest lists and friends who haven't met mingling, someone who would hate to have a party sprung on her if she weren't in the mood to party. It's become a hard rule if just for the fact that one surprise would seem to invite another. But lately I've been longing to shine up and reveal the part of my opalescence that would love to be showered and surprised by those who love me, and I have no idea how to ask for it. I've already picked my figs and set my boundaries. There's no way I can ask for something as small as this without changing everything.

Change is scary because it's concrete proof that, for all our choosing, we've never been in control and we can never relax. It's not just that an earthquake may strike at any moment no matter what we have planned for that afternoon. It's that there's more to us, to everyone, just below the surface, waiting to get out.

▼△▼△▼△

My first reaction to anything is that it's either good or bad, or something I want or something that was designed specifically to punish me and throw my life into turmoil. I long tried to find reasons why change has felt so uniquely terrifying to me. Is it because my mom and I had to suddenly move out of our apartment when I was thirteen, or because I was in Manhattan during 9/11? Was it because a whole semester of college was canceled because of Hurricane Katrina? Every time my life has been radically altered by things beyond my control, I've looked for the cause. But while I've relaxed to the idea of train delays and sudden death, I still cling to people, myself and others, as fixed beings. For a long time I thought this was because I was certain that people don't change; that the only thing you can trust is that people who attempt it will revert to who you've always known them to be. It's just easier to think of something, someone, myself, as an eternal truth.

But of course, people change, and my partner reminds me that anytime they or someone else I love has revealed a new part of themselves, I think they're going to leave me. It happens when friends move away, have kids, or choose a type of life I wouldn't choose. It happened when my partner lost weight a few years ago and began receiving more attention for their appearance, which at once made me feel deeply possessive and deeply aware of our cultural biases around body types. It happened when they started a job that made them happier and started relying on me a little less to provide the good in their life. And it happened when their presentation slowly started shifting, when they showed up to a date wearing eyeliner and I said it was sexy, and it *was* sexy, and then suddenly I couldn't feel the edges anymore. It happened in our long conversations about the nature of gender and masculinity, both of us trying to reckon with who we had been told to be and what we wanted, which fueled my fear that my partner would discover that what they wanted wasn't me. And it happened when I got their text on the way to work—"fuck, I think I'm genderqueer"—and even though I saw it coming from a mile away, and it was the closest I've ever been to feeling purely thrilled at a revelation, the voice crept in like water through floor cracks: this is it, I was just a pit stop of support and love, a fixed point against which they could define a part of their life before moving on to where they wanted to be.

Change seems like the wrong word to use for people. More often than not, when someone seems to change, they are just revealing a truth we weren't privy to before. When some thing changes, they might tell you to your face that it hasn't. They will assure you this is who they've been the whole time, deep down, and the only difference is the subtext is now text—a shimmering rainbow in the opal that has finally caught the light. Everything is the same, no one has strayed from the path. But even then my reaction is the same: panic. I feel betrayed, and while I'll act like it's the other person who has betrayed me, what I really feel is fury that I have clung so tightly to my sense of the world that I have no room for the wholeness of the people I love. I don't know the excitement of the new-to-me. All I know is the feeling of something bubbling up, the bursting steam and stinging heat hitting me in the middle of the night as I watch them sleep, same as ever before. Was this always true? Did I just miss it before? And if so, what am I missing now? What parts of them can't I see?

Sometimes it feels less like fear and more like jealousy, because I realize I feel fixed. I have had a list of things I am that helps me move through my world, not necessarily identities, but a set of data points I mistook for trends and facts. I have told myself I'm someone who writes, I'm someone who cares, I'm a lifelong New Yorker, I'm a hard worker, I'm mixed race, I'm a woman. As much as I'd resent anyone else for defining me solely by these terms, these were the neatly carved edges of my life, things I went back to when I lost my sense of self and needed to know what it was okay to be and to want. And I told myself these weren't just a few opalescent facets I was reflecting to the world. They were my whole self.

Lately I've been wondering what my edges really are, and finding they don't exist. I am someone who writes, but I don't have to be. I'm a hard worker, but it's something I've developed to shield myself from the profound laziness that seems to take over sometimes for no discernible reason. On rare occasions I think of what would happen if I left New York and realize, reluctantly, that I could make myself into the kind of person who would leave New York. I feel myself shimmer with every conflicting thought, my mind racing from wanting everything from everyone with no compromise. I'm cracking into a thousand shining pieces.

Change seems like the wrong word to use for people. More often than not, when someone seems to change, they are just revealing a truth we weren't privy to before.

At first, Kermit sounds like he's disagreeing with the premise of his first question. Sometimes I listen to "Rainbow Connection" and I hear a mocking tone in his voice, like he's imitating his detractors. Why are there so many songs about rainbows and what's on the other side when there is no such thing as an "other side" to a rainbow? They're a trick of the light that somehow bears the weight of our loaded, paranoid metaphors. But then, Kermit says those who say rainbows are only illusions are plainly wrong, and the answer to his question becomes obvious. There are so many songs about rainbows because wanting to see more, be more, is all we ever write about.

In 2010 a man named Paul Vasquez went viral for his video reaction to a double rainbow in Yosemite National Park. He keeps repeating "wow" and "whoa," unable to come up with more descriptive language because just look at it, it's a double rainbow! He's crying at some points, insisting that this vision must mean something and asking the universe to tell him. The video became a joke; some people laughed at his accent and stoner proclamations, and some probably found his enthusiasm heartwarming but were still amused by a grown man thinking a rainbow is cool. But when I watch it now, I nearly cry with him, the same way I do whenever I hear "Rainbow Connection," because he and Kermit seem to get it. I cry at the thought of finding beauty in temporality and change, of seeing a rainbow and not fearing that it'll go away. I imagine being thankful, not terrified, for whatever angle I'm standing at that lets me see a part of the rainbow, and grateful for the knowledge that there is always more to see, and that something so delicate and changeable has the power to exist at all.

Like a rainbow, the opal is created by water. It's a hydrated form of silica, an amorphous structure rather than a crystalline one, in which silica spheres are pressed together in a way that diffracts light from all angles. It is one of the most naturally captivating stones; a miner coming across an uncut diamond or citrine may not see much, but a vein of shimmering opal looks like the sun setting over the ocean in late summer. It looks like bioluminescence kicked up to the night sky from the sand. It stands out without a jeweler's touch. Opal's beauty is delicate, not delineated by any defined geometric shape, but more like a solid gel. It would not survive the tectonic movements that can be withstood by diamonds. But just because an opal can't survive as much pressure doesn't mean it's not strong enough to withstand some surprises. In 2008, the NASA Mars Reconnaissance Orbiter found opals on Mars. The hydrated silica was evidence to scientists that there had, at least at some point, been water on the planet. "We see numerous outcrops of opal-like minerals, commonly in thin layers extending for very long distances around the rim of Valles Marineris and sometimes within the canyon system itself," said Ralph Milliken of NASA's Jet Propulsion Laboratory. These minerals are proof that water existed more recently than scientists had previously thought, which increases the likelihood that Mars supported life. A planet we're still trying to figure out is a fitting home for an opal. It went from a dusty red nothing to a potential home. "The opaline silica deposits would be good places to explore to assess the potential for habitability on Mars, especially in these younger terrains," Milliken said. If Mars can be a home for something as delicate and changing as opal, maybe one day it could be a home for delicate, changing humanity.

I have many opals because it's my birthstone. I was born in October, under a sign known for mysteriousness, so maybe that's why the opal was assigned to this month. Scorpios are supposedly temperamental, jealous, loyal, calculated, sex-obsessed freaks. We contain multitudes, and all our traits and characteristics are already at the surface, ready to explode at the slightest provocation. What others see as change we see as strategic revelation. After all, rainbows have nothing to hide. Perhaps I am not a good Scorpio because it's taken me so long to understand this. But my true love for the opal is that it reminds me that stability can be a type of death. If it supposedly lets me see everything for what it is, it also urges me to see how quickly that landscape shifts, that it is not mine to build on. And that change isn't a betrayal, but a gift.

If there is a tarot for everything, the High Priestess card might be the card for opals. It traditionally depicts a woman sitting on a throne, a crescent moon at her feet, a dazzling curtain of wild pomegranates behind her. The card represents the veil between the conscious and subconscious, the gateway to the unknown that is no less real because it is hidden, and the journey to reveal both what we know and what we don't. And it asks if the reader is worthy of that knowledge. When describing the High Priestess tarot card in her book *Inner Witch*, writer and witch Gabriela Herstik wrote about the power of uniting all parts of ourselves. "Union of other and self is truth; both in the personal and the divine," she said. "This is also true of all the parts of ourselves. The sexual and the spiritual, the shadows and the light, the blooming and the wilting; the High Priestess reflects our divine multitudes back at us. Nothing in this world is one dimensional, and neither are we."

Sometimes I get a glimpse of this woman I could be, want to be, and am all at once, comfortable with the ebbs and flows of humanity, finding excitement rather than fear in the possibility of anything. Sometimes I wear an opal and think of her, me—a woman who may be one person one day and a different person the next, but who knows they are both authentic; who is welcoming of whatever version of herself she presents to the world and whatever others are and will be in return. I am the person Kermit sings that he and I and everyone is perhaps supposed to be. A person who knows that just because she can't see it all the time doesn't mean it's not there, that it is possible to be both solid and changeable. What a blessing to find the rainbow connection. What luck.

DIAMONDS
Aren't Special
and Neither
Are You

Diamond

DESCRIPTION:

Solid carbon with a crystal structure,
which can be clear or colored
depending on impurities within

COMPOSITION:

Carbon (C)

METAPHYSICAL PROPERTIES:

A symbol of strength and endurance,
as well as love and fidelity.
A stone to use when wishing
to attract perfection.

n South Africa there is a cave full of more diamonds than humanity could ever want or need. You won't get the chance to see most of them; few are flawless enough to enter the jewelry market. As the stones are excavated, carved, and judged by the four Cs—color, carat, cut, clarity—they are whittled down until only the most perfect remain. For color, white is optimal. For carat, or the size of the diamond, the bigger the better, usually. Cut depends on taste, but whatever you choose should be precise and symmetrical. A perfectly clear diamond is so rare "that it's possible to spend a lifetime in the jewelry industry without ever seeing one," writes the Gemological Institute of America, one of the organizations responsible for making sure no sullied stones poison the market.

Only about twenty percent of mined diamonds are of gemstone quality, and of those, a significant portion still have visible "flaws" or discolorations. Based on these statistics and these rigorous criteria, the diamond you might be inclined to think of, the one shimmering in the window of Tiffany's or on a newly engaged woman's hand, indeed seems rare. After all, it's the perfect stone, meant to represent the perfect relationship. How often would that come along?

"Perfect" diamonds may indeed be less common than their colorful, pockmarked counterparts, but diamonds are abundant. The criteria used to keep some from market was created to serve the diamond industry and changes whenever there's a need to unload product (think of every celebrity who has sported a yellow or pink engagement ring instead of a white one). The "carat," what so many have scrimped and saved to attain, is based on the size of a carob seed. Their brilliance is only revealed by precision cutting. And most people can't tell the difference between a real diamond and something like cubic zirconia anyway. A diamond's perfection and rarity, two things defined by their rigidity, wind up being arbitrary.

The story, and the myth, of the diamond is inextricable from the story of the diamond industry and the way the diamond has been advertised to the world since the 1930s. But that wouldn't have worked if the diamond didn't already mean something. These were the stones of aristocrats, and to have one meant to own a piece of light that could briefly lift you out of your station. And metaphysically, diamonds can do almost anything. Various sources cite them as a stone of love, psychic and physical strength, creativity, courage, and invincibility. Diamonds are a symbol of perfection, and having one promises you'll be made that much closer to perfect.

Perfection, too, feels special because it thrives on the illusion of rarity, especially when it comes to relationships—the very thing diamonds are meant to endorse. A singular person can achieve moments of perfection: a 100 on a spelling test, a just-cleaned house, even teeth, a just-cut gem. But even then, as soon as it's attained, it's dulled by the end of the pursuit, or overtaken by the anxiety of maintaining it. Perfection is harder to affix to a relationship, like a paper label sliding down an oily jar. If perfection is defined in part by its transience, then it seems anathema to something as permanent, and common, as marriage. The perfect diamond is a promise of the perfect relationship, because love is supposedly rare and so is this stone. The diamond's beauty is not in itself, but in that it beat out so many others to be here on your finger. And diamonds are still diamonds because we want to fall into the brilliant lie, no matter how contrived we know it is. We want the story that tells us our relationship is special. And we don't want to accept that rarity isn't all that meaningful.

▼▲▼▲▼▲

Until the nineteenth century, diamonds were rare. They were found mostly on riverbanks in India and polished until they shone, partially because of a taboo against cutting diamonds, which was believed to harm their spiritual potency. Tools to cut diamonds were first developed in Asia in the thirteenth century. In 1375, the first guild of diamond cutters was founded in Nuremberg, Germany, and the point cut was developed. Still, diamonds these methods produced were dark and dull, valued for their metaphysical properties rather than visual brilliance. As diamond-cutting technology advanced, so did the diamond's allure. At this point, diamonds *looked* valuable. Their popularity began to grow in Europe in the fifteenth century, with Agnès Sorel, mistress of Charles VII of France, wearing them around the French court, defying the sumptuary law of the time that regulated private expenditures. Mughal and Persian rulers collected massive diamonds, trading them among families, naming them after themselves and adorning their thrones.

The Koh-i-Noor diamond is a 105.6 carat stone stolen by the British East India Company and ceded to Queen Victoria. When you look it up online, what you first see is a set of glass replicas. Such replications of famous diamonds—the Hope diamond, the Pasha of Egypt, the Shah—were popular in the late nineteenth century as a way for the middle class to enjoy the beauty of diamonds without the cost. On an episode of *Antiques Roadshow*, one such set was appraised at up to $12,000 at auction. "It's quite a bit of money for glass," cracked the appraiser. Just the proximity to diamonds made it worth more.

The Koh-i-Noor has a history of being underwhelming. When it arrived in England in 1862 for an international gem exhibition, *the Daily News* was skeptical. Though the stone was "first and foremost in historic celebrity, if not in actual value," the *News* recalled how many people were "grievously disappointed" upon seeing the stone the last time around in 1851. "In its original Indian cutting, and taken out of its setting, none but a professional eye could judge of its hidden splendor." The Indians, who regarded the stone as the "prince of talismans," were apparently not good enough cutters for the Europeans, who deemed that their handiwork had ruined the stone's brilliant potential. But in 1852, the stone was recut according to European standards, reducing it from 191 carats to 105.6 carats. Some were horrified, but the consensus was that it was made more perfect. Yes, the stone was always impressive in size, but only by cutting away the flaws (and appealing to the sensibilities of a Western white audience) could it be made beautiful.

Diamonds like the Koh-i-Noor could draw crowds because, depending on who you were, you might not have seen a diamond before. But by the late 1860s, diamonds were at risk of becoming ordinary. Huge diamond mines were discovered in South Africa, flooding the market, making the gem available, and slightly more affordable, to anyone who wanted one. This was no way to run an industry that relied upon rarity, so the major investors created De Beers Consolidated Mines Ltd., a group that took control of the diamond trade to ensure "extensive price stability for the exporting countries and trusting companies." This is a nice way of saying they owned every aspect of the industry, including how many diamonds were allowed on the market, in order to perpetuate the illusion of diamond rarity—and keep prices high.

"Diamonds had little intrinsic value—and their price depended almost entirely on their scarcity," wrote Edward Jay Epstein in his seminal 1982 article for the *Atlantic*, "Have You Ever Tried to Sell a Diamond?" In it, he outlines how De Beers orchestrated a dual lie: that the diamond is rare, but also that the diamond is a symbol of commitment and love that no relationship should be without. In the 1930s, during the Great Depression, diamonds were seen as a luxury, and most women thought it absurd to spend money on one when so many more practical things could be had. De Beers hired ad company N. W. Ayer & Son's, which explicitly set the goal of creating "a situation where almost every person pledging marriage feels compelled to acquire a diamond engagement ring." The diamond ring, which was not a thing, became a thing. The slogan "A diamond is forever" became fact, and by 1951, eight out of ten brides in the U.S. were the recipients of diamond rings.

The campaign started with the assumption that the bigger the diamond, the better, and that two months' salary was a fair trade for the necessary privilege. But in the late 1950s, a glut of small diamonds was found in Russia, and De Beers had to change its sales strategy in order to control production. Suddenly, teeny diamonds on an "eternity band" for older women became a must-have. According to Epstein, "sentiments were born out of necessity: older American women received a ring of miniature diamonds because of the needs of a South African corporation to accommodate the Soviet Union." At this point, their ad campaigns focused on perfection at any size and emphasized that having a diamond at all was the important thing. In the 1980s, De Beers started a "He Knows How to Wear His Diamonds" ad series marketing diamond rings, bracelets, and cuff links to the sophisticated man who cared about his appearance and status. It featured tough men doing tough things—cowboys, skiers, stock brokers—aided by chunky diamond-and-gold accessories. It was a representation of a man's taste, his paycheck, and his ability to spend it on himself and not some woman.

In 2003, there was the "Raise Your Right Hand" campaign, encouraging independent women to buy diamond rings for themselves and reversing their traditional depiction of women as dependent consumers and men as providers; now, women should be celebrated for being independent enough to buy diamonds for themselves. The campaign featured women sitting with their legs splayed, staring straight into the camera, a diamond ring casting a flare so bright you could no longer see their hands. The left hand was for "we," De Beers said, but the right hand was for "me" and deserved to be spoiled on its own.

As I write, Le Vian's has been running an ad campaign for "chocolate diamonds" (aka brown diamonds typically reserved for industrial purposes), which promises the stones are "rare but affordable," creating a market for something that heretofore had been unworthy. Jewelry store ads now feature same-sex couples, couples with kids from other relationships, and other "modern" partnerships, which is almost enough to make most Americans forget about blood diamonds and bad press. The advertisers hope that you'll hope that your relationship, no matter what it looks like, will be good enough to warrant a rock someday.

The phrase "A diamond is forever" implies that a diamond's perfection is immovable and that it is up to the consumer to become worthy enough of one. The four Cs aren't just what make a good diamond; they are an eternal, objective standard. But De Beers knows that diamonds are only worth what they mean to the buying public, and De Beers's advertisers have chased those shifting goalposts as much as anybody, marketing them at any size, any color, any quality, as long as there's someone out there who thinks they're worth it. Diamonds may be in crisis again. Americans are waiting longer to get married, and progressive social politics have opened up the idea of who can get married and made people question whether or not marriage need be the end point of a committed relationship. The recession once again spooked a generation out of such an impractical investment. De Beers knows, maybe better than we do, that perfection is a moving target.

▼△▼△▼

Natural diamonds only exist because they have to. In the mantle of earth, where temperatures exceed 2,000 degrees Fahrenheit and the pressure is more than 725,000 pounds per square inch, the conditions change pure carbon's molecular composition into a different pattern. But you have to imagine that carbon, could it move, would. There is no path of less resistance for the carbon to slide toward. It becomes a diamond because there's nowhere else to go. It's romantic, if you squint. It's freedom from choice. All the carbon has to do is accept that it will now be perceived as rare and beautiful. That's what'll make it special. Otherwise it's just dirt.

▼△▼△▼

Diamonds may be stones for aristocrats, but to be a business they had to be both available for the masses and still rare, never reduced to being common. But it's hard to feel like the diamond carries that aura of rarity when your TV is flooded with ads from Jared and Kmart advertising diamond earrings for $59.99. Diamonds can now be made in a lab, cutting out the mythical and romantic origin stories. If the abundance of mined diamonds didn't kill the notion of rarity, the fact that humans can make them does.

I was convinced I was going to marry my first college boyfriend. I said "I love you" to him after a month, in awe that the first person I hooked up with in the dorm was someone for whom I felt this strongly. We can all have a hefty laugh now and say my love was more likely a combination of hormones and headiness from my newfound collegiate freedom, but when I close my eyes and take myself back to that moment in my twin bed in the early morning light, after having spent the night on my roof in the rain because of misplaced keys and miscommunications, shivering and wet and pressed together and finally about to get some sleep, saying "I love you" felt as real and true as saying it to my spouse.

When I said "I love you" I meant marriage, however far away. I fantasized about our life together. Though we were at college in New Orleans, we were both from New York, so it would be easy to move back and set up a life there. He was an economics major, and I was going to be a writer, and we'd live in an apartment with big windows and drink scotch (his favorite) and go to shows, and he'd finally quit smoking, and we'd combine our multicultural families and get a dog and maybe have one kid. For the next two months I held to this fact when my friends seemed unimpressed by him, when he sided with my roommate during a petty dispute, and when he told me he didn't love me anymore after we had sex. And when he dumped me, I cried, because now the plans I had made had nowhere to go.

Here's how you get a diamond for your beloved, or your ruler, according to stories told during the Tang Dynasty, which traveled from China to Cyprus. Go to the Valley of the Diamonds, a dangerous, sublime place, the type of place that could be considered beautiful now that we have the technology to not face certain death in the wilderness. Bring meat with you, either by killing an animal at home or finding one to kill along the way. (In fact, the latter is probably better so the scent of a fresh kill will be stronger.) Once you reach the valley, throw the meat down so it is pierced by the precious stones below. Circling eagles will, theoretically, be attracted to the scent of your kill and swoop down for the meat, carrying the diamonds with them back up to the cliffs. The myth doesn't specify how the prospectors were to wrestle the diamond-laden meat from the eagles. There's another myth that only goat blood could be used to cleave diamonds. Even in myth, diamonds were always a bloody business. Till death did they part, I guess.

According to Saint Hildegard, diamonds rise from the viscous matter of mountains and leave them split and weaker than they were before, apparently stealing all the mountains' strength. The stones could ward off evil, especially if they're ingested. Some people "have a harsh look" when they speak, she wrote "and at times they nearly go out of their mind, as if propelled by madness" before returning to normal and acting like nothing happened. The solution is to put a diamond in their mouth. Other scholars and philosophers across Europe and Asia credited the diamond with being both a poison and an antidote, a carrier of magic, a cure for bladder problems, a betrayer of inconstancy, and a destroyer of love if Saturn is in the right position.

(Maybe the diamond engagement ring is a secret trap, its power so overwhelming that it wrings the awful truth out of whoever is presented with it. A final test before forever sets in. *I trust that our lives will be fulfilling together*, it says, *especially in the presence of this sparkling threat*.)

"Diamonds make fools of the human eyes. Glassy and unappealing, unshaped and rough, diamonds can barely be distinguished from normal pebbles," say Eduard Gubelin and Franz-Xaver Erni in *Gemstones: Symbols of Beauty and Power*. "Only human rationality and technology can transform a diamond into a work of sparkling light." Almost a normal pebble, but not. Nearly unbreakable. Hard yet so clear as to be nothing at all. Of course every culture mapped their anxieties and ideals onto diamonds. They can be whatever you want them to be. The diamond's lasting myth is just that—it evokes fantasy. It's the stone to drape oneself in when gliding around in a red satin dress, men in tow. It's what heist teams heist, if only for the moment of opening a velvet-lined box to reveal piles upon piles of icy bits of light. And it's what gives power to a euphoric and terrifying question of marriage, and the fantasy that the term perfect could ever apply.

No perfect diamond exists without the work of a bunch of diamonds that were told they weren't enough.

I gave my partner a diamond ring and told them I was ready to get married. But it wasn't a proposal. The diamond had been passed to me by my aunt, which was passed to her from my great-grandmother—a bit of luck since we were the eldest or only granddaughters of our generations. My aunt had it re-set in a yellow-gold ribbon-esque setting, too big for me, but it sat in my jewelry box, ready for me to do whatever I wanted with it.

There was no first conversation about marriage with my partner. It had always been there, the assumed outcome from the moment we got together for the third time. The first time was in high school, so it didn't count. The second time, at twenty-one, I felt the weight of forever bearing down on my shoulders. It seemed obvious that this would be the ending, and I didn't want to go down that road yet, so I left on one of those around-the-world trips that's supposed to stuff you with enough "life experience" in six months to let you skip over the hard work of growing up. They left a key for me for when I returned, and I waited in their bed, eating boxed cookies they had left and listening to a playlist they had made, until my eyes rolled shut. I woke to them sliding into bed and enveloping me, and to the thought that I would never have to do anything else. Maybe I was like one of those chickens that needs a new chicken to be introduced to the coop while they're asleep, otherwise they'd be too aware of change and run away. But by morning we both knew where we were going.

When I gave them the ring years later, it wasn't that I had to tell myself I wasn't proposing to uphold a heteronormative idea of what a proposal should be. It didn't even occur to me that this was what I was doing when I walked over to their side of the bed, ring outstretched, and said that I wanted them to have this for whenever they were ready, because I was ready. My action seemed to be a practical prelude to the real thing. They needed a diamond to propose, and I had one. And as the woman, there was no way my ask was the real one.

Over the next few months I joked that if they didn't propose soon, I would, as if that was the most absurd outcome of our relationship and as if I hadn't already done so. A proposal—the right kind, the one in which I was being asked—would not change our relationship or our commitment to each other, but I wanted it all the same, and was deeply uncomfortable with that knowledge. I wanted something beautiful and special, and now I was scared I wouldn't get it, or that it wouldn't be as wonderful as I had been led to expect.

We've coupled love to marriage and we've coupled marriage to diamonds, and all three thrive on the assumption of rarity. What would it mean for love to be common? For marriage to become irrelevant as the benefits are made available to all in any combination? I say this as someone in love and in a marriage, who gets fiercely defensive of those things. But I could easily have married my college boyfriend if the terroir were right. I could have married anyone, which is not something I'm supposed to think about. We know love is not perfect, that it's arbitrary and common, that if we grew up a state away or spoke a different language we might not have fallen in love with the person we currently love, and in fact if we met them in a different context we might loathe them. But to admit that would be to break the spell and rebuild our relationships on . . . what exactly? Rarity is typically what makes something worthy, and I don't know how to value things if they are not unique. I don't know how to care about something if it's not special, and though I feel like my relationship is the only one of its kind, I don't know why that is.

Relationships become status symbols in their own right. Our entire economic structure is built on the idea that people will marry, and will produce children, and when those numbers start to go down people panic. Though it never would have occurred to me to say it, I had checked every box. At the time Matt identified as a man, and we lived together and had been together long enough that marriage seemed thoughtful and considered and not rushed out of lust. Our relationship, our love, qualified, and still I'm a woman who was proposed to with a fucking diamond ring. Just the way De Beers wanted it.

A proposal isn't necessarily a bad thing to want. As silly as the presentation of a diamond ring could be, occasion marks intention in a way a series of small conversations just doesn't. Asking someone to say yes or no in a life-changing situation grants the other person an awesome power. They're not being asked to go along with a suggested plan; they're being asked to decide. But as soon as a relationship becomes about living up to a set of outside criteria, it is divorced from its actual worth. It is no longer about serving and nourishing the people in it, morphing to their needs. It's about what counts and what doesn't count—what is of quality enough to be presented to the world and what must be hidden away so as not to taint reputations.

"Bad" diamonds are still good; they have use far beyond their potential beauty. They can grind down rough surfaces to smoothness. They can be made into thin membranes to cover openings in X-ray machines or enhance high-quality speakers. They are also used to cut the good diamonds, to form them into the perfect things ready to be loved and cherished by everyone. No perfect diamond exists without the work of a bunch of diamonds that were told they weren't enough.

The trick of the original myth of the diamond is that it says it's about rarity when it's actually about effort. The valley was full of diamonds. A diamond is valuable because it requires a hike to a remote valley and the serendipitous arrival of the eagles. It's not just that they exist, but that they inspire such planning and daring to aquire. The trick of the current myth of the diamond—that they are singularly, objectively beautiful—is that it takes effort to make them so. It is in the hands of a master diamond cutter that a glassy stone becomes a radiant heirloom. It is the action that makes it special.

In his memoir *Once More We Saw Stars*, in between the harrowing narrative of the death of a child, author Jayson Greene describes the moment he met his wife, shocked that he remembers it at all. He says it wasn't necessarily love at first sight, but more as if an outside voice came down to him and lit him up, an immaculate conception of love telling him, "This is important. Pay attention." I was furious when I read those words, because I'd used the exact ones to describe the moment my partner and I met, both in oversized black band T-shirts, me squinting slightly in the sun, knowing I should also introduce myself to the guy next to them but unable to stop looking at their face. *This is someone to remember*, I thought, *find them again*. I wasn't ready to be presented in such plain terms how average my feelings were.

Diamonds are, if anything, stones of order. Their structure is a forced, rigid tetrahedron, and its rigidity is what makes its beauty possible. Their magic is a logic puzzle: if you find the right river stone and if you treat it a certain way then you will have a diamond; solve for love. But turn your typical love story—the world aligned so that we met on this day, at this spot, in these moods, and we knew we could never be apart—upside down, and it turns to chaos. Because a minute later, a different first sentence uttered, a different outfit or attitude, and you very well could be married to someone else and perfectly happy about it. It didn't have to be my spouse. I could have spoken to someone else first and heard that disembodied voice. The pattern that led to us was forged after the fact; we could look back and say that from the beginning it was always forever. Love just sounds better when it's written as preordained, because that way, if you don't have it, it's because it's an impossible thing to have. The Koh-i-Noor is easy to judge from a distance for its imperfections—you'll never own it. It's something reserved for the perfect and rare who somehow have all of their shit together enough to invest in the feeling. There must be order and scarcity, something else controlling all of this, otherwise what's your excuse? Abundance has never guaranteed equal distribution, but things as deep and strange as love or wealth or identity are not of the realm of "deserving" or "earned."

I have told myself my marriage is different—unlike everyone who crows about it in Instagram captions, we are actually best friends, we actually have been through thick and thin and know more about each other than we know about ourselves. Surely, all other married couples must be kidding on some level. They must have something to go through the rigamarole of staying together for so long, but no one has what we have. With my parents divorced, you'd think I'd only view marriage as a lie. But because I never thought it was necessary, I figured it was something to do only if it were truly worthy of my time. Why do anything unless it's the best version of it? We are the only ones who got it right.

Your marriage will never transcend the institution, but you want it to feel like it will. Marriage is special, so special, but also so common, and to reach the state where it starts sounding like a good idea and not a prison, it has to feel different from the mere idea of marriage. It has to feel like the two of you cracked something open and are scamming the system, and yes, you're technically getting married, but clearly this is something grander and deeper than the law ever scratched. There's no way, you tell yourselves, this thing you're doing, that billions of people have done before, is ordinary. And getting to that point takes effort, not happenstance and coincidence.

The love that you build a marriage on is lying at the bottom of every valley, at the back of every cave, amply dull, waiting for someone brave enough to make the journey and bring the right tools. Diamonds, the perfect stone, are not scarce, and neither is love. It can show up in any size, hidden under any mantle, forged in the worst and weirdest conditions. The point is the choice to make the journey. What if diamonds were more special the more we had, and seeing one on someone else only confirmed to both of you how wonderful your shared accessorizing was? I'm trying to let my diamond make me as common as it is, part of a world in which caves overflow with unimpressive pebbles just waiting to be shined up and sold. I do not want my sense of self to be based on what others do not or cannot have. I want to be as abundant as perfection.

OBSIDIAN
and Finding the Truth Beneath the Surface

Obsidian

DESCRIPTION:
Naturally occurring volcanic glass
that is formed from quickly cooled
lava. Black and opaque in color,
with a high shine.

COMPOSITION:
Mostly silicon dioxide, with
magnesium oxide and iron oxide
(SiO_2, MgO, Fe_3O_4)

METAPHYSICAL PROPERTIES:
Used for divination, allowing the
user to see deeper truths and
subconscious thoughts

The rumor goes that in 1770, England came close to passing a law allowing a man to divorce his wife if she had used makeup to convince him she was prettier than she really was. Whether she did it "by scents, paints, cosmetics, washes, artificial teeth, false hair, Spanish wool, iron stays, hoops, high-heeled shoes or bolstered hips," she could be tried for witchcraft and her punishment would be justified, because— well, look at her red lips and smooth skin. Who looks like that?? She's obviously a liar.

If the law sounds like a myth, that's because it is, or at least it's an inverted version of a story told in Irish, British, and Norse mythology. In the story of the loathly lady, a haggard old woman is shown kindness by a young man and reveals herself to be young and beautiful. The story is happy instead of scary because her face changes in the right direction—natural beauty is the ultimate reward. No one is suing their wife for being suspiciously pretty without lipstick.

There is no proof that the Hoops and Heels Act of 1770 existed. In a law journal article from 1971, "The Law Passed by Everyone but Parliament," D. Dean Willard found no evidence that the House of Commons or the House of Lords ever considered such a bill. But I'm less surprised that people want to believe it existed than I am at the possibility that it may have been fake all along. Everything about it feels real, from the hypocritical insistence that women wearing wigs was deceitful but men's powdered hair and heels were an acceptable form of self-presentation, to the assumption that a woman's worth was tied to her beauty, which both must exist and be natural. Even if it was never a law, many women have been punished for it anyway.

No matter how much progress Western society has made in its attitudes toward makeup, beauty, and fashion, the undercurrent of this cultural conversation is that these things aren't "real." But neither are our physical traits. Our bodies? Malleable through age, tattoos, surgery, accidents, and fluctuations in our weight. Our voices? Easily changed by habit and hormones. Our senses? Again, subject to age and accidents. We need physical form to exist but our bodies are not us—or at least not the totality of us. What we project to others is always partially a choice, one that's treated as an unfortunate inevitability of living in a society that requires social interaction and clothing. The assumption is we'd all strip down to the "real" if we could. At least, that'd be the virtuous thing to do. How déclassé to want to draw attention to oneself any other way. How gaudy to declare your desire to be seen.

▼▲▼

Obsidian is hot, violent lava that cools into inky glass with sharp edges and a reflective surface. It's used to pierce through skin as a spearhead or blade and through perceptions as a scrying stone, which allows you to see your past, present, and future stripped of all the gloss. According to Pliny the Elder, obsidian was used as a mirror, though it wasn't great at the job. "It is dull to the sight, and reflects, when attached as a mirror to walls, the shadow of the object rather than the image." It's this quality that lent obsidian the metaphysical property, recognized across multiple cultures, of being a literal black mirror. The fractured nature of our psyches! The duality of man! It's all there in the stone. If it doesn't show you your exact self, it must be showing you something deeper, a "real" you beneath the face you sell to the rest of the world.

Whereas pyrite makes you aware of an outward and an inward self, obsidian is used to make you confront what you have been hiding from others, or from yourself. "This beautiful and powerful stone can help cut through the drivel, shatter illusions, and uncover lies," one gem website claims. "It can help you remove any blockages in your being and see through the facades." In its surface, you're supposed to find deep truths that maybe you're too scared to admit to yourself; the tough love side of self-care. But what is truth depends on what's considered dishonest, and on who is passing judgment.

I don't remember feeling the need to wear makeup for men. That's not to say the influence wasn't there, but who could possibly unearth subconscious motivations during puberty? Makeup was what my mom wore sometimes, and what her friends wore more often, and therefore what I figured was—like drinking alcohol and paying rent—the realm of adults. You don't do it to make yourself look better, I thought; you do it because you're a grown-up.

While middle school involved some silver eyeshadow and sticky lip gloss, eighth grade was when I got serious with an Urban Decay sparkly black eyeliner pencil. I didn't know how to apply it just to my lash line, so I settled for filling in my entire eyelid, leaving it raw and tender

Obsidian is hot, violent lava that cools into inky glass with sharp edges and a reflective surface. It's used to pierce through skin as a spearhead or blade and through perceptions as a scrying stone, which allows you to see your past, present, and future stripped of all the gloss.

from glitter abrasion. The first time I did it I didn't quite recognize myself, but I told myself that was the point. Children don't wear eye makeup, and I was no longer interested in being a child. If a teenager is who I wanted to be, this is how I needed to look. My appearance told a story, and I was aware of what my choices said to those who looked at me, and about my relationship to the things I didn't choose. After all, I didn't have to wear eyeliner, but being a girl who wore dark black eyeliner carried a set of other definitions, ones I hoped would be applied to me. Perhaps now I'd be seen as punk, or cool, or rebellious, not a child who was into her American Girl dolls for far longer than was probably healthy.

Costume is another word for lie, but just because I wasn't yet the rebel I wanted to be didn't mean my look wasn't authentic. I chose what I wore, how I presented myself, because I liked how dark eyeliner and ripped jeans and old T-shirts and studded belts looked and felt. Frilly blouses felt unnatural, but my black sweatshirt covered in pins and buttons felt like me, whoever that was. When I looked in the mirror, I saw both sides of the reflection: the person I was and the person I wanted to be—or at least as close to that person as you can get when you're fifteen. No outfit perfectly bridged the gap between perception and reality.

The word *glamour* comes from the Scotch, who altered the word *grammar*, which was associated with the mysterious art of studying literature. A glamour was a spell of perception, first understood as magic to affect the subject's eyesight. In 1721, the Oxford English Dictionary cited a glossary of poetry that said, "When devils, wizards or jugglers deceive the sight, they are said to cast glamour o'er the eyes of the spectator." Later, a glamour became a sort of influencing charm specifically tied to getting what you want by making yourself beautiful. To be glamorous was to be so bewitching, so alluring that you were in complete control not just of what your subject saw of you, but how they then reacted. And that came out of a control of yourself.

In her essay "Thoughts on a Word: Glamour" for the *New Inquiry* in 2012, Autumn Whitefield-Madrano described glamour as a checklist of items that unlocks certain treatment if we can tick each box. There are appearances we culturally agree upon to mean something more than just what they are, such as red lipstick as the sign of a vamp, white cotton as a sign of innocence, or a suit as a symbol of a woman's embrace of masculine power. "It's not hard to get glamour 'right,' but since glamour is a set of references—a creation instead of a state of being—you do have to get it right in order to be seen as glamorous as opposed to pretty, polished, or chic," she writes. It is literally a spell, a collection of ingredients when, mixed in the right way, produce an otherworldly outcome. "We don't stumble into glamour; we create it, even if we don't realize that's what we're doing. Call glamour a performance if you wish. It's equally accurate to call it an accomplishment."

▼▲▼▲▼

Central Mexico lies on an active volcano range, prime ground for obsidian production. That, plus the lack of metal ore in the area, means that obsidian was and is omnipresent in Mesoamerican societies, influencing how tools were used, how society was structured, and how spirituality was interpreted. If volcanoes were the homes of the gods and ancestors, obsidian was, in a sense, the bricks and mortar of those homes. In Maya and Mexica cosmology, obsidian was associated with darkness and cold and offered in conjunction with stones representing light and life. In the Tarascan state, it was a stone of omens and bad dreams but also of power. It embodied the patron deity Curicaueri, who was literally "in Tarascan political-religious praxis a chunk of obsidian from which knives were knapped that would then be carried forth to conquered towns," according to David Haskell in his article "Tarascan/Purhepecha Monarchs as 'Stranger Kings'" for the University Press of Colorado's website in 2018. The mineraloid was both symbolic of power and powerful itself, a representation and the real thing.

In Aztec mythology, Tezcatlipoca is the lord of the night sky and of smoking mirrors. He observed the world through the reflection of his obsidian foot (his real one was chomped off by an earth beast when he and Quetzalcoatl created the world). He was the god of fates and the patron god of Aztec royalty, who used obsidian mirrors to pierce the veil between mortality and the gods, a conduit for the gods' messages. But the royals didn't just reveal Tezcatlipoca's will to the people, they revealed the truths of the people, especially those they'd rather hide, to the gods. Obsidian mirrors were affiliated with Tezcatlipoca and allowed the Aztecs to both see and be seen by their master of fate. He revealed himself to humanity only when they revealed themselves in return.

Obsidian was also a healing stone, pulverized and applied to the eyes to clear cataracts. "This 'vision sharpening' quality of obsidian may have been a contributory factor in the origin of beliefs concerning the all-seeing nature of Tezcatlipoca, the acknowledged 'night vision' of his jaguar alter ego, and the divinatory power of obsidian mirrors," writes Nicholas J. Saunders in "A Dark Light: Reflections on Obsidian in Mesoamerica." He continues: "In this way, perhaps, the Aztec (and probably pre-Aztec) use of obsidian directly affected the sense of vision, and thus perceptions of the world." Obsidian may not be a good functional mirror, but they offer other ways to help us see.

The terrifying thing about any god or spirit or partner is the idea that there is an entity that sees beyond what I present. Some people call that love and find it comforting, but I can't stop the alarm bells from clanging in the back of my head when someone close to me tells me something they consider obvious about me, though I've done nothing to present that truth. That they've seen beneath my mask is taken as proof of the power of their feelings, but also often spoken of as "knowing the real me," and the dichotomy between facade and "real" usually ignores why that facade was put up in the first place. Maybe it was to falsely gain something, but more often my performances are for protection, or to fit in, or to evoke something in myself that doesn't quite exist yet, or it does exist and I just want to show it off. The problem isn't that our facades mask our selves and must be stripped away in order for us to be close to family or lovers or god. It starts much earlier than that, in the thinking that such a binary even exists. Instead, the self is just as fluid as anything, existing at various points between what we do, what we feel, and what we want.

The most famous version of the loathly lady story is "The Wife of Bath's Tale" in Chaucer's *Canterbury Tales*. In it, the wife of Bath tells the story of a knight who rapes a young woman. King Arthur is about to put him to death, but Queen Guinevere pities the knight and says if he can figure out what it is all women want, he will be free to go. In his searching he finds an old woman who promises to grant him the answer in exchange for whatever she wants in return. He returns to the court and reveals that what women want is sovereignty over men, something it would have been nice for him to know before he raped the maiden. In exchange, he finds he has to marry the old woman.

On their wedding night he is repulsed by her, and she asks whether he'd prefer an ugly but loyal wife or a beautiful but unfaithful one. Remembering the lesson he learned just recently, he said it was her choice, at which point she rewards him for clearing this very low bar by transforming into a beautiful *and* loyal wife. Beauty here is not just a reward for a job well done on the knight's part, but a fundamental truth about his wife. This kind, wise, and forgiving woman is now as beautiful outside as she is inside, as if physical appearance should be a manifestation of inner truth, and as if it's naturally correlated with youth, smooth skin, and radiant eyes. Why couldn't her wrinkles be a sign of virtue?

There is a reason we want to cut through the veil. Appearance alters the perception of everything that comes after. Humans trust beautiful people more, and we don't listen to those we deem ugly. According to a Procter & Gamble study, as reported in the *New York Times* by Catherine Saint Louis in 2011, choice of clothing and makeup "increases people's perceptions of a woman's likability, her competence and (provided

The problem isn't that our facades mask our selves and must be stripped away in order for us to be close to family or lovers or god. It starts much earlier than that, in the thinking that such a binary even exists.

she does not overdo it) her trustworthiness." In a 2018 article for the *New York Times*, Eva Hagberg Fisher wrote about choosing outfits for court dates and other events related to a sexual harassment complaint she filed against a professor at the University of California, Berkeley who had harassed her for three years. She had to balance projecting that she was a grad student and also a capable adult, a victim and a strong woman, "just plausibly sexy enough to look like [she] could have been harassed but 100 percent [wasn't] asking for it." She mitigated a series of false assumptions with black turtlenecks and loafers and hair tied in a low bun. In 2018, the university suspended the professor.

Of course, Fisher should not have had to do this. The third-wave feminist recontextualization of women's makeup and clothing says these are not tools of the patriarchy, but individual choices of self-expression. Women, and people of any gender, are free to wear what they want, for any reason. And they should! Equating makeup with competence is utter bullshit. But there's a recent backlash to that idea because it doesn't take into account what other people will interpret about your appearance regardless of your intention. Our appearances, what we want to look like, are influenced by the perceptions of those around us. No, Fisher shouldn't have had to play into this notion, but what would have happened if she didn't?

▾▴▾▴

Here's a quick lesson in astrology: In the zodiac, we have our sun signs and our rising signs. If you've ever looked up your horoscope, you know your sun sign. Our sun signs represent our basic personalities, our inner boss, Who We Are when We are at our most Us. However, if you've ever looked up your horoscope you're probably also familiar with the sensation of it getting you completely wrong. If you're supposed to be a mysterious Scorpio, then why do all your friends think you overshare? If you're supposed to be a headstrong Aries, why do your coworkers think you're the one who goes with the flow?

Those who don't believe in astrology say it's because it's a scam, which, fair. But believers often cite rising signs as the culprits digging the ditch between what we put down and what others pick up. Our rising signs are supposedly the masks we present to the world, the way everyone else perceives us regardless of who we are and what we want. There's a difference between who we are and who everyone else is seeing. But at some point, the mask can become real. If everyone treats you as the masked version of yourself, on some level that's you. And if that's who you want to be, all the better.

Even people who insist they don't give a flying fuck about appearance want to signal something sometimes, whether it's the effortless cool of the perfect bedhead, or the "don't talk to me" of large headphones on public transportation. (Even when we want to be ignored, there's an outfit for that.) Women who don't wear makeup are signaling just as much as women who do, whether it's that they're too tired to use it, they're rebelling against societal pressure to use it, they physically can't, or that they're "above it." Even a lack of a facade is sometimes a facade. And the facade we present to the world isn't a direct matter of cause and effect. There are more forces at play, both internal and external.

It may be possible to go through life without ever encountering this gap between presentation and identity, to always be read and understood exactly how you want without having to compromise a single part of your appearance. You choose your makeup, your hairstyle, your outfit, and you waltz into the world and are seen and known exactly the way you planned it. Lucky for you; please let the rest of us know how that works. Because for most of us there are times where that divide makes itself known, when our glamours don't work. Sometimes it comes as a surprise. Other times, it's entirely expected. There are glamours we put on ourselves to show the world, but there are also glamours the world puts on us, spells that affect how we perceive ourselves and others that come from outside sources—history, government, prejudice, fear. We can't even see ourselves clearly. There's always a layer of dark magic.

When the witch looks into her scrying stone, what she's looking for is honesty. There is something there—a shape, a voice—that reveals a truth that reality can't. The art of scrying implies reality is a lie that must be seen through, and is in fact a substitute for the truth.

I did not choose to be mixed race, nor did I choose to be a cis woman. That isn't to say I wish I could have chosen against those parts of myself (I quite like being both these things), only that they are factors of my identity that are outside of my control. The color of my skin, the texture of my hair, the certain shape of my eyes or lips that signals to people that there is something nonwhite about me, the general presence of my womanhood—these aren't things I chose. But they are facts of my appearance that affect me, whether it's in subtle microaggressions or institutionalized racism and sexism.

In "Ideology and Ideological State Apparatuses," Marxist philosopher Louis Althusser illustrates his theory of interpellation with a hypothetical scene of a policeman calling out to a passerby on the street, explaining how a call from the police pulls its subject into a relationship with the law. All it takes is a policeman shouting, "Hey, you there!" for the passerby to be transformed from an independent individual into a subject of the police, whether he has done anything wrong or not. We police each other's outward identifiers every day, turning each other into subjects of our own interpretations. With these forms of identity, the observer makes the call, and we are subjected whether we like it or not. These are the glamours that are cast for us. Because no matter how we style our hair and choose our clothes, other people will come at us with their own conclusions. Our race, our gender identity, our sexual orientations and disabilities and body types and sizes allow others to categorize us without our permission.

There are days when I "dress up" as Indian, which I know is not actually what's happening but that's often how it feels, because my Indianness is usually something others can only see if aided by the right accessories. I put on gold filigree earrings or bangles, I choose embroidered scarves. Sometimes I'll wear a bindi and tell everyone that I'm trying to "decolonize" it, and I am, but I'm also scanning the room and watching an anxious timeline unfold in which another Indian person (or hell, a white person) accuses me of cultural appropriation because they don't think I'm actually who I am. I would have the exact same genetic mix if I never wore gold, or bindis, or silk. Plenty of Indian women don't. I know who I am, and I know that others' perception can't take my identity away from me. There are days when I pay parts of myself no mind. I know they are there, and that's enough. But sometimes, I need to know everyone else knows. What good is an identity if you can't be identified? I want an identity that not only I see.

▼▲▼

Metaphysically, obsidian is also used as a shield. It is said to block negativity and provide protection, so its user can obtain clarity of mind without so many external influences. According to the crystal website Charms of Light, it "helps you to know who you truly are." When we dress up, when we experiment, sometimes it's because we are trying to obtain that clarity of mind and discover who we are. But sometimes it's because we already know, and we have nothing to hide. Our presentations aren't masks but mirrors, an invitation for others to see exactly who we are.

I try to not look at what we have done, as a species, as proof of what we will do or should do, but the fact is, in thousands of years of human history, everyone has expressed some interior aspect of themselves with their exterior presentation. I doubt anyone has ever passed another fully clothed human on the street and simply thought "ahh, a human." We have dressed up. We have made ourselves things to be looked at. Between the exteriors we're born with and the exteriors we construct, it seems like it'd be easier if we just stopped assigning ulterior meanings to everything. And clearly there are many places (particularly with those things we don't choose) where we should. Existing in public becomes an effort in calculation that vacillates between being joyful and terrifying. Will they see what I want them to see? Will they focus on this over that? Will my glamour work, or is everyone else's more powerful?

Can you tell this is personal? I don't know why I have always been so desperate to be known. I assume it has something to do with the endless questions about where I'm from. *No, where are you really from?* But to tell the truth, I was doing this before I learned to think of my race as a condition. I remember turning my butt to a stranger in the hall of my apartment building on Halloween, pointing and bellowing, "I'm not a bunny, I'm a LAMB," to a woman who dared confuse my costume for the former. I know it's not the deepest identity crisis, but I was incensed for at least the next two doorbell rings.

But there are moments where the glamours fall within your control. When the things you've internalized about bodies, gender, race, age, and abilities burn away like morning fog, and you put on the things you want to put on, and there you are. Exactly the you *you* want to be and the you *you* are. We can't control it all; we know we will still be categorized. But we try to have a say in those categories because the moments when we glimpse what our lives could be like if we felt that way all the time are the ones we live for.

Obviously I'm not the first person to point out the connection between presentation and identity, or that our appearances are masks and also facets of ourselves. Philosophers and artists have devoted a lot of time to the ego and subconscious, to the actor who only reveals himself while playing a role. But much of the conversation around appearance tends to land on the idea that we shouldn't care. We're still buying the idea of not judging the book by the cover, that appearance is incidental to the person underneath it. But while appearance is not the only thing, it's not nothing, and in denying its importance, we deny each other those moments of agency. When you treat the facade as a false self, you miss what it's trying to tell you.

Ultimately, the drive is to rewrite the checklist. To have our glamours say what we want and not what others have learned to interpret through prejudice, colonialism, or just plain misunderstanding. To bring what we see in the obsidian to life. Our appearances become synecdoche for ourselves, a shorthand for the things we are proud of and the things we are scared of and the things we might not realize we're projecting. But when we like how we look, it's because, consciously and unconsciously, all these spells are at work.

How we perceive each other is all we have. We cannot intimately know every person on earth, so we rely on this shorthand for communication, for understanding. That's why it feels so important, and that's why we keep reaching for the obsidian in spite of the calls that insist it shouldn't matter. Not because we're too vain to think about more important issues, or because society is forcing our hand. We do it because there are things we need to communicate in order to survive and thrive. We do it because what would life even be if we could not be seen? Block out the negativity, look into my reflection. No matter what's in it, it's telling you the truth.

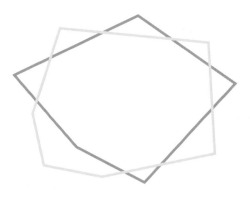

AMBER,
Death, and the
Preservation
of Life

Amber

DESCRIPTION:

Fossilized tree resin, usually clear
yellow to orange in color, and sometimes
with animal or plant inclusions

COMPOSITION:

Carbon, oxygen, and hydrogen
(C10 H16 O)

METAPHYSICAL PROPERTIES:

Thought to possess life energy.
Good for healing, and for
connecting to past lives.

You might have learned about amber from Mr. DNA. The 1993 blockbuster *Jurassic Park* included a pseudoscientific interlude in which the characters take an informational tram ride through the soon-to-be-opened theme park and a cartoon double helix explains how they were able to bring dinosaurs back to life. "One hundred million years ago, there were mosquitos, just like today" he explains, bouncing around the screen, "and just like today, they fed on the blood of animals, even dinosaurs."

But then, occasionally, a blood-bellied mosquito would land on a resin-covered tree and get stuck, coated, hardened, and buried, and millions of years later would still have that belly full of dinosaur DNA.

A day before *Jurassic Park* was released, scientists extracted fragmentary strands of DNA from a weevil that had died while being engulfed in tree resin 130 million years before. It was believed to be the oldest DNA ever found, and it set off a race of research with the promise of rebuilding ancient animals—possibly even dinosaurs—dangling at the finish line. There was just one problem. The DNA was highly susceptible to contamination, absorbing other DNA from mold spores and bacteria and the scientists themselves. No one could replicate the weevil. Then, in 2012, scientists discovered that DNA has a half-life of 521 years, meaning it would cease to be readable after about 1.5 million years. And even without all that pesky science, the dinosaur DNA from *Jurassic Park* would have rapidly broken down during the mosquito's digestion, making it pretty impossible to have survived even a couple of hours, much less eons. There was no way *Jurassic Park* could be real. But what a tempting story, that all the secrets to our past are sitting somewhere perfectly preserved.

Amber doesn't quite feel like a gem. It's too light, like it's made of plastic. It feels odd that something so insubstantial was allowed to survive; surely it should have crumbled by now. It's made of tree resin, which is different from sap. While sap is like the blood of the tree, carrying nutrients up from the soil and through the branches, resin exists only to protect the tree from outside invaders. When a branch breaks or a bug tries to claw its way in, the resin seals and sterilizes the injury and prevents further damage. Amber's metaphysical properties are some of the most literal given what the resin is physically capable of. Everyone from the ancient Romans to the creators of Chinese medicine expanded on the idea that amber has the power to heal. "Worn upon the neck . . . it is a cure for fevers and other diseases, and, triturated with honey and oil of roses, it is good for maladies of the ears," wrote Pliny the Elder. "Beaten up with Attic honey, it is good for dimness of sight; and the powder of it, either taken by itself or with gum mastich in water, is remedial for diseases of the stomach." It could also keep one safe from harm, both in life and in the afterlife; ancient Roman graves have been found with bodies adorned in amber to protect the soul on its journey.

But amber also has the property of preservation, which leads some to believe it can heal not just your body but your soul, and the souls of everyone who has come before you. It connects you to "ancient memories of your wisdom, truth, and purpose" and can mend past traumas that you didn't even know you were carrying with you. More than other gems, amber is recognized for its connection to life. The tree it came from has most likely gone extinct, but the appeal is that some part of its life, a moment of the day that resin was formed, is still perfectly preserved inside. When it warms it releases a scent, an experience of something long ago captured. Amber's magic says we can see the past just as it is, perhaps live in it for a moment. It is a physical manifestation of hindsight, holding the promise that if we could just go back, the moment would be there, clear as day, and we could fix things, change things, or just remember why. It is so easy to get trapped in that sticky promise.

▽△▽△

Death is supposed to give life meaning. Life, as the more fleeting of the two, is really the state of not being dead. Life might be marked by decay and movement toward death, but it is still movement. And life without decay, or an eternity of stasis, is just another version of death, as we've learned from every tale of everlasting life, from *Tuck Everlasting* to *The Good Place*. This is to say amber is just like us: fluid and moveable one day, and then rigor mortis hard the next. It's pretty obvious that amber should represent life and death. Its warm, golden hue evokes the sun and its life-giving shine, as well as the knowledge that one day we won't feel it on our skin. A bee or mite trapped inside hardened amber was once alive but is now suspended in a state of life-like death, transformed into something hauntingly beautiful. Something ends when amber forms it's a reminder that death will always come no matter the quality of one's life.

American schools are fond of referring to ancient Egyptians as "death obsessed" in middle school curricula, as if that were an insult, but they seem no more so than any other culture with a robust ideology around the afterlife. The premise of any afterlife is that life, in some form, will continue after death. Some traditions are more abstract about this than others. In Hinduism, the soul is reincarnated as many times as is necessary for it to understand its completeness, after which it joins the cosmos. In Mormonism, there are three realms in which a person may reside for eternity, depending on their religious beliefs on earth, with all of their baptized family. Outside of organized faith, there are ghosts that linger on earth, stuck in the houses where they were wronged, replaying the same moment, needing to make peace with the past before they can move "on," wherever that is.

In Ancient Egypt, amber was considered the tears of the eye of Ra, the sun god, who represented life, growth, and creation. Amber and pine resin have been found embedded under the skin of mummies, supposedly to protect them on their journey to the afterlife, but also because pine resin is antibacterial and helped prevent decay, ensuring the body wouldn't fall apart before the soul's journey was through. In this mythology, after an arduous schlep through the underworld, the weighing of the soul, and rebirth, souls would be reunited with their bodies and together enter the Field of Reeds, where the Nile was always flowing and the crops always came in. For all the journeying and inter-action with gods, the ultimate reward was the nicest possible version of the most boring parts of existence: farming, eating, spending time with loved ones, all while wearing the best clothes your family could afford to put in your coffin. An eternal replication of what you did on earth, a forever of good harvests and good health.

Not all afterlife myths are so literal, but most promise a preserva-tion of something you already know or can easily imagine. Heaven is freedom from earthly pain and frustration while hell is an abundance of it. Eternity is your family reunited, all the things you wanted but never got now available for the taking, the ability to talk to all the famous people you thought were cool, the peace of being able to farm and harvest without worrying that there will be enough, because there is always enough. This, of course, depends on how good you are in life, whether you follow the rules and arrive at your judgment with a sinless heart and a light soul. But the reward for getting it right is largely the same—your life, better, continued.

Even when considering an afterlife outside of religious traditions, we have a hard time envisioning anything but an augmented earthly bureaucracy. In the 1988 film *Beetlejuice*, the dead are given a handbook that reads like "stereo instructions," and hell is the DMV. In the 1991 high-concept rom-com *Defending Your Life*, the Egyptian soul-weighing morphs into a courtroom drama where the recently deceased are given a lawyer and must prove to a panel of judges that they have lived their lives without fear. Everyone is decked out in comfy robes and shuttled around office parks and hotels during their downtime. You can eat as much spaghetti as you want and not get fat. You can replay the highlights of your life on TV. There are meetings and appointments and schedules to keep to. Everything is carpeted.

In the sitcom *The Good Place* the audience is convinced, at least for the first season, that heaven looks like a cute suburban neighborhood, where everyone eats frozen yogurt and fondue with monogamous soul mates and sometimes you can fly. There are houses and restaurants and parties and interpersonal dynamics to navigate, and people still go jogging for some reason. The reveal is that [SPOILER ALERT] what we thought was heaven is actually "the bad place," something you could easily have figured out if you thought about the continued presence of cul-de-sacs in eternity. Life in the neighborhood is in fact a form of torture that forces people to continue to operate in polite society, down to the pressure to be in love with their so-called soul mates. The main characters go in search of the real Good Place, or at least a "medium place" where they won't be flayed and burned. But even when they get close to the Good Place, it seems like nowhere anyone would choose. Sure, it smells like cookies and everyone is guilelessly enthusiastic, but they're also all wearing polar fleece.

The visions of the afterlife presented in these stories probably aren't what any of their creators believe really happens after we die; but an abstract, interdimensional landscape free from anything resembling human interaction or emotion doesn't make for compelling, plot-driven entertainment. But so many of our thoughts of life after death are wrapped up in not just our anxieties about dying, but also our anxieties about life. Death becomes freedom, but not too much. A soul joining an all-knowing ball of light is too weird for daily contemplation. But the best version of these afterlives (not the jogging) is a comforting wish. A nice house with all your childhood pets, or reliving your wedding day, or finding yourself preserved in the happiest moments of your life—if you have to die, that doesn't sound too bad.

It's only when I'm really happy that I feel like dying. When life feels fully saturated and the only possible place to go from here is down and muted and dimmer. I don't really want to die, but when I'm fizzing and filled with gratitude for the privilege of life, I'm overcome with the melancholy wish that things could always be like this. I'll be lying on the couch after a deliriously happy day when I remember it will be bad again, someday, and I say I feel so good I want to kill myself. This is not a thing people say! The first time I admitted it was on the phone at two a.m., and the person on the other end immediately threatened to call the police. It probably should have occurred to me how I sounded, but the thought felt so natural that I assumed everyone else felt the same way. I assured my friend that it's not really true, that'd I'd never do that, life is grand. But for me, cresting on the wheel of fortune doesn't inspire acceptance that what goes down must come up again, that just as it will be bad again, it will be good. Instead, I feel my buoyancy disappearing.

Really, I just want it to snap off. An afterlife that resembles life on earth, with work and needs and people to answer to, sounds exhausting, and an eternity filled with my highest moment would only dilute that moment. Instead, I want it all to freeze, a beautiful time had by all petrified so fast no one notices, no one even has the time to mourn a lost future. Everything preserved at the best moment, not the worst.

But so many crystals are women's pain, hardened and celebrated. In Ovid's *Metamorphoses*, Clymene, daughter of the ocean personified, bore the sun god Phoebus (also known as Apollo or Helios) seven daughters and one son, Phaethon. Phaethon is mocked for being unable to prove his parentage and begs Clymene to tell him the truth. She assures him Phoebus is indeed his father and that he should travel to his Palace of the Sun and see for himself. There, Phoebus tells Phaethon his mother has spoken the truth and promises to give his son anything he wants. So Phaethon asks to drive his father's sun chariot for a day. His father warns him of the fire-breathing horses, the terrible heights, the rushing and turning sky. "No doubt, since you ask for a certain sign to give you confidence in being born of my blood, I give you that sure sign by fearing for you, and show myself a father by fatherly anxiety." But Phaethon can't be persuaded to choose anything else.

Phaethon was so small that the horses thought the chariot was empty. They dove toward the earth, scorching the land, destroying cities, evaporating seas. Earth herself was choking, and she commanded Jupiter, "Look around you on either side: both the poles are steaming! If the fire should melt them, your own palace will fall! Atlas himself is suffering, and can barely hold up the white-hot sky on his shoulders! If the sea and the land and the kingdom of the heavens are destroyed, we are lost in ancient chaos! Save whatever is left from the flames, and think of our common interest!" Jupiter was forced to strike down Phaethon with a lightning bolt before he could do further damage. It is a myth of hubris and anxiety, of a son wanting his father's acknowledgment and approval so badly he cannot see he already has them. Often, the myth about the grief that comes after is ignored.

After Phaethon is killed, his mother wanders the earth looking for her son's bones, and his sisters cry. They cry so much that when the eldest tries to throw herself to the ground she finds her ankles have stiffened. They cry so much that one's hair turns to leaves, another's legs become wood, and Clymene tries to save them by tearing the bark from their skin. "'Stop, mother, please' cries out whichever one she hurts, 'Please stop: It is my body in the tree you are tearing. Now, farewell.' and the bark closed over her with her last words," wrote Ovid. "Their tears still flow, and hardened by the sun, fall as amber from the virgin branches, to be taken by the bright river and sent onwards to adorn Roman brides." Everyone else in the story gets to move on. Phoebus still carries the sun across the sky, Clymene returns to the oceans, the world moves. But the sisters are reduced to hardened tears, forever captured in a state of grief.

There are more myths. In a Lithuanian legend, the goddess Jurate lived in an amber castle under the sea. She fell in love with the mortal fisherman Kastytis, and after they are both punished for their affair, Jurate cries, and her tears mix with shards of her castle and wash up on the shore. (Jurate lives in the Baltic Sea, the site of the world's largest amber deposit.) In *Othello*, as he is about to kill himself over his grief, Othello refers to himself as a man "whose subdued eyes,/Albeit unused to the melting mood,/Drop tears as fast as the Arabian trees/ Their medicinable gum." Amber is not just proof of life, but proof of trauma, and whether directly tied to death or not, the idea is that tears are curative. A tree's resin only appears when it is hurt, and in our love of humanizing the inhuman, we probably saw in a tree the cathartic release of a good cry. The hope is that by letting it out and putting it somewhere else, we will heal. The crystal shop House of Intuition's website describes amber as "a gentle healer, cleanser, and transmuter of negative energy of all kinds on all levels" and says it's good for healing and depression. If amber is the pain of a long-gone tree frozen in time, then maybe it can represent the same for anyone who uses it. Cry into the amber, let it fossilize, and move on.

Not all resin can become fossilized amber. It needs the right conditions. Most of the time, the resin washes away after it's secreted, never getting a chance to harden. Only certain forms of resin are resistant to sun, rain, bacteria, and fungi, and even then it needs to find itself buried in wet clay or sand to fossilize without too much oxygen. There is little reason why some resin is preserved, taking along whatever particles are trapped within, and some resin dissolves in the rain. As much as humans have ascribed meaning to amber—these pieces are here because it was Jurate's castle, these are the tears of a mourning woman—like most things in nature it's a total crapshoot.

If amber can heal our traumas by connecting us to the past, it's with a magic that says dwelling on those moments isn't just a masturbatory exercise. It helps us recognize our past traumas, perhaps generational traumas, that sit like stones in our stomachs. By looking at them from every angle we're supposed to see what they're doing to us, whether their presence is a balm or a festering wound, and protect ourselves from a psychic attack if it's the latter. Amber says that by taking time to obsess over trauma or memory or death, we can move on and perhaps even learn something. But Phaethon's sisters probably did not want to become amber-sobbing trees, no matter how gracefully Ovid wrote them to accept their deaths. If it had to happen, and if it were up to them, they might have chosen a different day to become trapped in. Maybe a nice afternoon while their brother was still alive. Maybe some future day that they never got to see. But they can't control it; they're trapped on a loop, doomed to relive the same moment forever.

Often we have no choice over what stays with us and what gets washed away. Moments like death, marriage, and birth are intentionally memorialized through ceremony. But we also live through horrible traumas and unspeakable joys, and those too are transcribed on a part of our soul that doesn't forget, does not fade with time—a repository of moments we wish to live in forever, and moments we'd sooner cast to the bottom of the sea. Amber reminds us we are supposed to choose what we carry forward, but it's also a warning not to get too bogged down. Death is coming no matter what, but there will be time enough to relive all those moments again and again and again.

The preservation properties of amber also mean we don't have to throw the past away, at least not yet. We can keep looking at it, keep analyzing it, and turn to it when we need to escape the here and now. Sometimes it feels so good to live in the past, and now it's easier than ever. My Facebook reminds me of things that happened three, five, or twelve years ago without my prompting. My Gmail is an archive of flirtations from college. With the help of the internet, I can be the teen complaining about her friends not getting along like they used to. I can be the twenty-one-year-old caught between two dramatic loves, writing impassioned letters back and forth, remembering when life was chaotic and unpredictable and I didn't know where I'd end up. I can be someone with a fuller face, flatter abs, stronger arms (but admittedly with a worse haircut). I read and relive that part of my life in excruciating detail, every kiss and text that was ever documented like it is happening in this moment. We're meant to look at these moments preserved in metaphorical amber briefly in order to make sense of the present, but what if you stayed?

I've set guards against the temptation to become too enamored with my past life. I've deleted select emails and done my best to focus on the present, where these loves are married or absent or have just moved on, where my body is what it is. I pull myself out before the warm orange sap takes me whole.

I think often of Kurt Vonnegut's Tralfamadorians, the creatures who exist at all times simultaneously, who can focus on inhabiting and observing as many frozen moments as they'd like without the emotional burden of the unknown. They are powerless to prevent anything from happening, so they throw their big green hand up and say "so it goes," living in the moment, or at least a moment, whichever one they feel like. When they meet Billy Pilgrim in *Slaughterhouse-Five*,

The preservation properties of amber mean we don't have to throw the past away, at least not yet. We can keep looking at it, keep analyzing it, and turn to it when we need to escape the here and now.

he is like any other human—afraid of what comes next, traumatized by what has happened to him, and convinced that there was another outcome possible if he could just figure out where it all went wrong. The Tralfamadorians laugh, and eventually Pilgrim adopts their fatalistic view of the world. After all, he has been "unstuck" from time, doomed (or blessed) to visit past and future moments of his life, though without control over where and when he goes. When Pilgrim says "so it goes" to the humans around him, he means to reassure them there is nothing we can do except to enjoy the moment we're in, even if horror surrounds us in all dimensions.

But I'm sure, when he returned from the Tralfamadorian zoo, his friends and family found him an unrelatable asshole, creepily content with death and tragedy, so understanding of the big picture that he forgets about the small ones that make a life. At its best, amber might make us time travelers to our own lives, but at its worst we become either stuck or unstuck, so myopically focused on one moment or so disconnected from the passage of time that we can no longer sense its flow.

It's easy to make an afterlife of life. You can relive a moment, beautiful or painful, so convincingly that you forget anything else has happened since. You could mimic what you've already done to the point that you become a ghost, haunting the same spots and performing the same rituals over and over again instead of moving on. The past is that dead mosquito preserved in amber, too full and comfortable to know it was being carried on a gummy river to its death—but at least it's a known quantity. At least we don't have to contend with the discomfort of surprises. Or so we think . . .

In *Jurassic Park*, the scientists thought they knew what they were doing. The dinosaur DNA was incomplete, so they fused it with modern frog DNA under the assumption that they could bring back dinosaurs *and* control them. Obviously, that didn't work. The frog DNA allowed the dinosaurs to spontaneously change their reproductive organs, they started laying eggs, and life found a way. The scientists didn't know all of what had happened, so they couldn't know what would happen.

Because no matter how many mosquitos were trapped in amber, they couldn't fully know the past. Not the details, not the things that would make the presence of dinosaurs in a human society so truly awesome.

Ever since DNA was discovered, we have spoken in metaphor of things inherent to us as "encoded in our DNA." There are things we can't change and things we are predisposed to, inevitabilities that would be foolish and unproductive to fight. Things that have happened. We have relied on the thought that it has all been written, and that's all there is to read. But there are some moments available to us and some that aren't, and some that were but will never be with us in full, colorful detail no matter how often we turn to amber for help. When I want the world to go away, I have to remind myself that I have been pleasantly surprised. If the world had stopped when I asked it to, or if I decided one perfectly preserved moment was the only good one there would ever be, I would have missed so much. Sometimes it feels easier to be trapped, but I don't want to forget about the sun on my face.

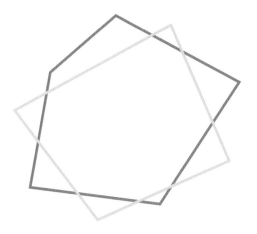

AMETHYST,
For When You
Seek Balance
at All Costs

Amethyst

DESCRIPTION:

Purple quartz, which attains its
color through the presence of iron
and other trace elements

COMPOSITION:

Silicon dioxide (SiO_2)

METAPHYSICAL PROPERTIES:

Encourages balance and moderation
in one's behavior. A stone of
peace and calm.

F reelancing takes you to weird places. When I was a freelancer (and I write this as someone who currently isn't but will, in all likelihood, find myself doing it again) I was often asked what my "beat" was, and my joking answer was "whatever I'm paid for." I say joking because delivering the line with a smile diffused the tension with people who had salaries or built careers step-by-step. But for most, freelancing is about staying afloat. If I was gaining new skills or making new connections, it was usually an afterthought. I'd write for most publications about most subjects, as long as you paid me. This is how I agreed, on assignment, to go to a senior center in

Queens, New York, to interview its patrons about their superhero fantasies while they had their portraits taken. I started the day doing the same thing at a center on the Upper East Side, interviewing around twenty people about their lives, their heroes, and the things they wanted in their wildest dreams. But their dreams weren't so wild anymore. Most just wanted to be young again, to be able to walk around without pain, to have their memories back. Nothing so extreme as turning invisible or having superstrength. Regular strength was good enough.

By the time I got to Queens I was exhausted, having tried to keep up cheery, inquisitive tone for longer than I can typically manage. It was probably obvious that I was developing an attitude. So I shouldn't have been surprised when, in the middle of asking one eighty-year-old woman what kind of superhero she'd be, she cut me off and asked (or declared), in a thick Cuban accent, "You're a water sign, aren't you?"

Was it that obvious I was emotional and increasingly miffed? I said yes, I'm a Scorpio. Most people forget Scorpio is a water sign. Scorpions don't live in the water, and Scorpios, so the stereotype goes, don't revel in their emotions—they weaponize them. A brown, shiny sting when you least expect it. Water, sure, but as a sharp blade of ice.

"What you need is an amethyst," she said. "For protection."

My Didu has told me the same thing over the years. Though she is a PhD who had a long career as a biology and zoology professor, she still puts her faith in the stars sometimes, reminding me that my birth chart predicted my digestion problems and imploring me to eat more yogurt. She's a Capricorn and prefers her birthstone, garnet. I was born in October; shouldn't I be wearing more opals? No, she said, an amethyst; preferably a ring.

The word *amethyst* comes from the Greek for "not to intoxicate" and was said to protect wearers from becoming drunk. Ancient Greeks wore amethyst talismans and drank wine from amethyst cups, hoping the trick would work and they could indulge themselves without consequence, though I'm sure it didn't. But maybe telling ourselves we're protected, balanced, that we're in control—even as we slosh and scream and bask in amethyst's violet—is almost as good as the real thing.

There's more than one way to feel intoxicated. The amethyst is not just a talisman to ward against chemical intoxication; it's also meant to keep you from getting drunk on emotions. Soldiers wore these stones to keep a clear head. Bishops put amethysts in their rings to signify their sober spirits, dedicated and steady. These were not people who were supposed to lose themselves. Did their amethysts represent protection or a promise? Would their bodies have been a hospitable home for drunkenness without the stones? Either way, the potential of amethyst is control at all costs, and for those who buy into amethyst's powers, emotions are barriers to truth, rather than harbingers of it.

▼▲▼▲▼▲

A few years ago, my partner, my cousin, and I took mushrooms and headed to Golden Gate Park in San Francisco, skipping with anticipation, mistaking every breeze or goose bump for the beginning of the trip. We lay in a field and felt the sun warm our faces. We talked about our relationships and dreams. We marveled at a red-tailed hawk that landed by a nearby stream, that now we all insist was the size of a man. I felt sun-dazed and happy, but nothing near high.

Then, chaos. There was a cannabis festival in the park planned for that day (we forgot to check the calendar, and if we had, we would have seen 4/20 looking back at us and known what was up), and hundreds of people began filing in as a DJ played bad reggae. My companions, well into their trips, panicked, and I grabbed their hands and did my best New Yorker weave through the throngs until we were safely out. I was a clear-headed warrior, and if the psilocybin was ever going to take hold, it wasn't now. If I didn't move, I don't know whether either of them would have taken the lead. How lucky, I thought to myself, that I was responsible and sober enough to act. That I was in control of myself.

Later that afternoon, after the drugs wore off and we all decided we needed a nap, my partner recalled how good it had felt—like you could close your eyes and feel the trees breathe. At the time I was working across the street from Central Park, and during my lunch hours I would take last night's leftovers to a bench and eat while overlooking the pond, then take my heels off, walk through the grass to an even, dry spot, and lie in the sun, taking care to tuck my shift dress so it wouldn't get too wrinkled. I would close my eyes and, without any effort, find my breath in time with the wind, my cells swaying with everything, eyes tearing as they opened, some half hour later, to a bleached-out landscape as the sounds of tourists and other lunch breakers filtered back in. *But that's always how it feels*, I thought as my partner recounted what sounded like the happiest moment of their life thus far. *That's just what it's like to be outside.* I felt superiority and loss, like I already knew this but somehow missed the epiphany that makes the knowledge mean something. I stared at the ceiling, furious that the drugs seemingly hadn't worked and even more furious that I was mostly feeling relief that I was never at risk of being out of control of myself. If I wasn't going to feel out of control, what was the point? Why couldn't I just let myself enjoy this? I fell asleep crying.

I'm not trying to brag about not needing substances to feel transcendence, only noting that my emotions are taut behind my face like a meniscus curve. In this way I am rarely sober. Small feelings turn into obsessions, moods into Moods, thoughts into crying fits. In high school, I wasn't cool enough to be invited to parties where there would be drugs or alcohol, so I told everyone I was straight-edge anyway, that I didn't even want to be there. My white lie made unpopularity feel like a statement, but it was also a convenient excuse. I didn't want to use most of the substances that were making the rounds; I was afraid of what they'd let out. I didn't need any more help to find the edge of control.

There are certain people who relish telling you their drinking stories, or relish in hearing them. I began to drink in college, the sort of binge drinking that makes for a good laugh if you still enjoy stories where the climax is always someone puking, passing out, or being so out of control that they very nearly do something irreversibly dangerous, but are saved last-minute before the comedy turns into a tragedy. In one, I am naked and blacked out and staggering to my door, saved by my roommate who, still awake and studying, argues me down from my insistence that I'm heading back to the bar, and that, not to worry, they have shirts at the bar. In another, I've drank so much artificially colored wine that I climbed over the gate to the college pool at four a.m., ripping my skirt in the process, to go skinny-dipping. In another, I'm wandering through a national park on a weed brownie, halfway hallucinating and sadly resolved that this is my new reality, so I just have to get used to perceiving everything like this from now on. These stories are only compelling, and even then not very, because they are not the norm.

My telling of these stories has changed, to "thank god I'm not like that anymore" from "oh my god let's do it again." But it doesn't take much for me to tell them. Staying balanced is a virtue, but at some point it changes from desire to command. Go too far, warn the voices, and you'll never come back. You can't be too much, or you'll lose yourself. When I tell these stories, I'm testing the waters. I'm trying to prove to myself I can unhinge and survive.

▼△▼△▼

On the Cartoon Network show *Steven Universe*, Amethyst, one of Steven's otherworldly guardians, is unhinged. She is short for her kind due to having remained underground for an extra five hundred years while the rest of her kin were born, permanent proof that she is off-balance. At the beginning of the series, she's just the wacky one. She eats gross things grossly, pulls pranks, changes shapes, and is strong but impulsive. Her behavior looks a lot like comic relief, and it is, because it's a cartoon.

Things are bad enough. There's no logic in choosing to be more vulnerable. There is so much of oneself to lose. The goal, then, becomes to find stability without sacrificing the thrill of emotion, letting the unhinging happen without setting up camp on that planet.

But later, we learn Amethyst is just trying to right herself, as if there is an objective center she is desperate to reach. She was born on Earth, so she lacks a connection to the culture and history of her people. She feels jealous and inadequate about anything and everything. She cares too much and not enough about the wrong things in turn, and when that's pointed out to her, she lashes out, because everything she does is an attempt to just be the thing she's supposed to be. The deep sadness of Amethyst is that it never quite works. Even when she decides to embrace that she is not who she should be, she does so out of spite. It takes the entire series for her to realize who she is.

After shopping for crystals one day, my partner asked me if the magical properties assigned to crystals had anything to do with the characters' personalities in *Steven Universe*. In general, they line up pretty well. Rose quartz is full of unconditional love. Pearl is gentle and pure. Garnet is useful to have in a crisis. But amethyst made me think this was a fluke. If Amethyst the character is anything, she is perpetually intoxicated, swinging between flagrant confidence and deep insecurity, like she is just one more tequila shot away from passing out. She isn't even-keeled. She is mania.

Before *Steven Universe* there was another myth about amethyst, and she was innocent, no matter how the story goes. Dionysus, the ancient Greek god of wine and fertility and celebration and madness and carnality, lusts after a maiden named Amethyst. She refuses him and prays to Artemis to remain chaste. In a different version of the story, Dionysus has just been insulted by a mortal, and drunk, whether on wine or his ego, vows to set tigers against the next mortal his caravan bumps into, who, again, is Amethyst on her way to pray to Artemis. In both versions, Amethyst calls out to Artemis for help, who sadly concludes that the girl has to die one way or another and turns her into a luminous white stone. Better than being raped or mauled by tigers.

Regret is easier to face when there is no one left to ask follow-up questions, and after seeing what he'd caused, Dionysus repented. In one version, he pours his wine over her stone form as an offering, dyeing her purple. In another, he cries so hard his tears form a stream around her and her stone body soaks up the water, which has mixed with the wine in the dirt. Both Dionysus and Artemis move on with their lives, duty-bound to the ideals they represent. Amethyst remains frozen in time, a sober pillar for others to look up to, or to carry with them as her body inevitably crumbls and embeds itself in the ground.

The amethyst is a common stone, caused by the abundance of silica and quartz that's present at every stage of rock formation. Its purple color comes from radiation from iron impurities, but the color is unstable and can be changed easily through heat. Apply enough heat and it turns into a yellow-brown citrine, a stone not of balance but of abundance. It can even fade in the sun. Its changeable qualities might be why Pliny the Elder was skeptical of the Greek claims about amethyst, writing in his *Natural History*, "The falsehoods of the magicians would persuade us that these stones are preventive of inebriety, and that it is from this that they have derived their name." But it's not just the Greeks that have named the amethyst the stone of calm and balance. In the Chinese feng shui tradition, it's meant to calm excessive emotions, to cool the head and leave you clear to receive bigger, better blessings (namely, wealth). In the Middle Kingdom of Egypt, the stone had associations with "domestication of wild things from the desert margins, the harnessing of ambiguous powers for good, the safe traversal of dangerous liminal states, the establishment and maintenance of Maat, fertility, and the nurture of young children," writes Laurel Darcy Hackley in "Amethyst, Apotropaia, and the Eye of Re." The stone was mined in Egypt's Eastern Desert, where, in the story of the Eye of Ra, the feminine Eye wandered after leaving the masculine sun god Ra, angry and needing to be tamed. The "odd color of the material suggested a strange origin, between worlds," the place in the desert where the day met the night. Eventually, the Eye is tamed and returned.

All these myths have made amethyst the modern stone of substance regulation, of protecting its wearer from Dionysus-like destruction.

The Amethyst Initiative is a movement to combat drunk driving by lowering the drinking age in the U.S., and to promote moderation and responsibility, which the amethyst symbolizes. Amethystics are the class of substances that can block the absorption of ethanol, helping the user to sober up or not get so drunk in the first place. The stones were worn by women worried their drunken husbands would beat them, and by those who feared becoming "overly passionate" in their love, still under the impression that abuse was a matter of too much love. In all these associations, the amethyst represents a restoration of order. Everything will be fine, as long as we can meet in the middle.

Maybe it's as simple as the way colors relate to each other on a color wheel, purple lying between passion-sparking red and cooling blue, not too much of one or the other. A hue defined by its lack of extremes.

▼△▼△▼

I spend a lot of time reading stories of drug use online. I search Reddit for tales of mixing substances gone awry, someone taking DMT and acid and having the psychedelic waves interfering at the wrong amplitudes. I read through message boards of junkies giving each other advice on the long-term effects of amphetamine use, on how to shoot heroin between your toes instead of in your arm, all the tips and tricks to stave off the comedown, confessions of regret about ever trying the benzos that made so great. I read and reread the parts of memoirs where people hit rock bottom. I know Cat Marnell was fifteen the first time she tried cocaine and that the song that was playing was "Fame" by David Bowie. I know Drew Barrymore poured Baileys over her ice cream when she was seven. I know Robert Downey Jr. smoked pot with his dad at six.

But on the rare occasions when I've been offered harder drugs (and sometimes just when a joint is being passed around at a party) I feel my cheekbones tense with forthcoming tears, the tension of curiosity and fear not knowing how to express itself in any other way. Fear has always won, which is a deeply uncool thing about me. I can pretend it's disinterest or moral objection, and sometimes those are in the mix, but when a friend casually offers me a bump at a bar, or tells me about a lovely romp on molly, or when the room fills with sour smoke, all I want to do is run.

The most I have let myself enjoy is a painkiller, and that was only to let it do its job, and only after a hard fight. I had lopped off a piece of my thumb at a party while using a mandoline to slice delicate petals of apple for a tart. "It's easy," I told the host, who would be taking over the duties any second, "and there's a guard, but you don't need to use it." A minor god of mischief was summoned by those words, and as they left my mouth I felt the cool air brush over a part of me that should have been on the inside. A trip to urgent care and a chemical cauterization later, I was back at the party, laughing with adrenaline and waiting for the inevitable crash when the lidocaine shot wore off and I had to figure out what to do next.

It was excruciating. Beats of electric pain shot up my arm. I could barely form sentences, and although the doctor had said to take Tylenol, it was clear that wouldn't be enough, so my partner presented me with Percocet left over from their collarbone surgery a year before. But I only cried harder, that familiar fear slicing through my delirium like coffee in an empty stomach. I refused—the doctor hadn't said it was okay, I'd been drinking that night, and what if I get addicted? We're in the middle of an opioid crisis, for fuck's sake! "You're in pain. This is what you're supposed to take these for," they insisted. A logical, balanced suggestion. I swallowed half a pill between deep sobs.

I spent the next week on the couch popping pills and watching Bollywood movies, embarrassed that a cut so small could lay me flat. But between the guilt of not being able to work and that of having allowed myself to become infirm in the first place (guilts that need to be examined but not now, surely there are better things to do), I tried to enjoy my daily high. I let the tabla soundtrack course through my body, let myself become hypnotized by the high synthesizer strings. I wondered whether I had hallucinated a plot in which a dog is possessed by the spirit of Krishna but nope, that was in the movie. And mostly I relished in the moments when I stood up from the couch, feeling like I was on moon gravity. It was fun, and the second I let that thought streak through my head it was chased down and carted off by shame. How dare I enjoy this unnatural state. I'm too vulnerable, I'm out of control. In this compromised position, I need to be taken care of, and that way lies danger.

When Greeks drank wine from amethyst cups, it was to reveal the truth that drunkenness is said to bring without revealing its twin weakness. A loss of control means a vulnerability to attack, and when enjoying yourself means putting yourself in danger, any precaution is worth a shot. After my week on the couch, I've relaxed a little about the pills, occasionally taking one to sleep after I've thrown out my back or wrenched my neck out of place. But each time, the guilt of willingly becoming so vulnerable for such a brief pleasure crawls back. Would an amethyst protect me from the fear of losing control? Would it let me breathe and accept that balance is sometimes not a state of perpetual calm, but an averaging out of large emotions and experiences? Or would it just sober me up and tell me that maybe I'm right to be afraid? For my experience to be enjoyable, I would have to trust myself and my surroundings, trust that nobody is out to get me. I'm still working on that.

Alcohol appears to be the only substance I can handle, letting myself feel the loosening and tingling of intoxication while staying in control, for the most part, until the bartender offers me a shot for the road. But everyone I know is giving up drinking. After all, it is terrible for you. If someone is reading this book in twenty years, I wonder where this trend will be, if it was just a phase or if alcohol is to a new generation what chewing tobacco is to mine—a deep signifier of time and place that nobody is interested in picking back up, even for nostalgia's sake.

The state of affairs at the dawn of the 2020s is leaving everyone feeling raw already. Things are bad enough. There's no logic in choosing to be more vulnerable. There is so much of oneself to lose.

The goal, then, becomes to find stability without sacrificing the thrill of emotion, letting the unhinging happen without setting up camp on that planet. The options so often seem diametrically opposed: calm or chaos, sobriety or an irretrievable loss of self. And for some people, yes, addiction changes what "balance" means in that realm, where abstinence needs to be the tool. But there are so many other places where moderation just means the death of two beautiful extremes instead of one.

Balance, moderation, calm—these are the things we are warned we should want, that we are told are the paths to success. No one is selling meditation apps trying to make us more agitated, more emotional. Peace is supposed to come through control. Feeling the right things at the right times, in the right amounts. Never tipping the scales. But it has only recently occurred to me that balance is not a fixed state. I'm sure even the bishops in their amethyst rings lost themselves on occasion. What would their faith look like if they didn't let a spirit take over once in a while? What would soldiers in amethyst breastplates do in battle if not for will and pride? These are not places for measured behavior.

Drugs or not, I am not good at keeping my feelings in. Sometimes I can hold them tight, but more often they race out of me like pus from a pierced blister, formless and gross and impossible to accurately name. I am so bad at judging what needs to happen when. When I should be more judicious, I burst. When I should be open, I find myself breathing in through my nose and out through my mouth in that way that heats the back of my throat and makes a noise like a radiator, so my partner has to ask me what's going on and why I won't just tell them what's wrong. Where others have scales, I have a pendulum, and it's taken all my energy to make its trajectory smaller and smaller, the recovery shorter, until you can barely see it move.

I never asked my grandmother, or the old woman in Queens, what the amethyst should be protecting me from.

I also never questioned why balance is something to aspire to. Maybe it's one of those things that, as a woman, I just accepted was an accurate judgment of my behavior—too emotional, too quick to panic, hysterical. It's not true of all women, but for me, sure. I know what control looks like, and I cultivate it at every turn. But there is a mood I get in when the air is right, sometimes sober and sometimes not, when I let myself burst, and any reaction to it is more fuel for my flame. I race down streets and hug with force and sing in the faces of my friends, my laugh ricocheting off buildings. I rise to dares and fizz with charisma. I thrive on some unseen energy. I bring the party with me, and not even the occasional side glance, not even the sense that this would be insufferable behavior if I indulged in it all the time, can invite the shame in. It's a mood that is worth protecting. I would never want to replace it with whatever a more moderated version looks like.

Maybe these women simply saw my Scorpio shell; the ice crystallizing in my veins; the way I stop and smile and keep everything back even while my eyes shoot fire. Balance by force. Control by desire. They knew that true balance is not always a midpoint between two extremes, but the ability to visit each with the confidence of knowing you'll return. The amethyst can remind me that no matter how far from myself I seem to be, I'm not lost. It will protect me from the curse of moderation. Maybe this rock will be what I need because it'll show me how to crack open and let the pendulum swing.

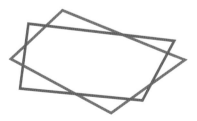